MW00982061

CASTLES
OF THE WORLD

One Hundred Historic Architectural Treasures

MALINI SAIGAL

WORTH PRESS

Contents

Below: Leeds Castle, England.

First published in 2010
by Worth Press Ltd

Concept, editorial, layout,
and design
© Worth Press Ltd 2010
www.worthpress.co.uk

This book was created by BookBuilder **B.**

Editor: Nirad Grover
Design: Malini Saigal
DTP: Arun Aggarwal

All rights reserved. No part of this publication may be reproduced or transmitted in any form or by any means electronic or mechanical including photocopying, recording, or any information storage and retrieval system without prior written permission from the Publisher

Every effort has been made to ensure the accuracy of the information presented in this book. The Publisher will not assume liability for damages caused by inaccuracies in the data and makes no warranty whatsoever expressed or implied. The Publisher welcomes comments and corrections from readers, emailed to info@worthpress.co.uk, which will be considered for incorporation in future editions. Likewise, every effort has been made to trace copyright holders and seek permission to use illustrative and other material. The Publisher wishes to apologize for any inadvertent errors or omissions and would be glad to rectify these in future editions.

Maps are for indicative purposes only and do not claim to represent authentic international boundaries.

Floorplans throughout - Copyright reserved for each individual castle.

British Library Cataloging in Publication Data: a catalog record for this book is available from the British Library

ISBN: 978-1-903025-99-4

Printed and bound in Singapore by Imago

A LORD'S HOME IS HIS CASTLE

The Medieval Castle was the product of the Feudal system and its primary function was twofold – domestic and military. Lordships of the military aristocracy received land and castles from the king or superior lord to inhabit, protect, control and manage, in return for allegiance and military service or labour. The Feudal society was divided into three estates: the clergy, the nobility and the workers. Each estate (rank) was obligated to those above and below it.

CASTLES–
ARCHITECTURAL
ELEMENTS & STYLES

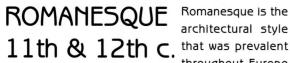

St. John's Chapel, in the White Tower is the most perfectly preserved early Norman ecclesiastical architecture to survived in its original state.

The White Tower was the first of many Hall-Keeps to be built in England. The Tower of London, 11th century.
BELOW: Illumination of the captured Duke of Orleans, who was held in the White Tower, c1415.

Traitor's Gate, the river entrance of the Tower of London

ROMANESQUE 11th & 12th c.

Romanesque is the architectural style that was prevalent throughout Europe in the 11th to the 12th centuries. As the name suggests, Romanesque architecture grew out of the classical tradition of ancient Rome and its various revivals in subsequent centuries. Themes such as the semicircular arch, the apse, the stone tunnel vault and belfry towers were developed. Richly decorated motifs from nature were represented in stone on different styles of column and pilaster capitals.

NORMAN 11th & 12th c.

The Romanesque style of architecture arrived in England with the Normans and is referred to as 'Norman'. The Norman Conquest of England in 1066 by William the Conqueror, was followed by an intense building activity. Two types of building predominated – the Castle and the Church. The Castles offered protection against revolt and served as feudal residences for local lords. The greatest of William's royal castles in England is the White Tower at the Tower of London. Build in 1086, it was the first stone castle in England.

Lichtenstein Castle, Germany. Rebuilt in in the Neo-Gothic style in 1840–42 on the site of a 13th c. castle, which was totally destroyed twice before. Lichtenstein – its name in English means 'light (coloured) stone'.

A picturesque castle gatehouse with tiny twin observation turrets, a wooden drawbridge over a deep ravine – is the perfect setting for a romantic Neo-Gothic experience of the fairy-tale kind.

Crow-stepped Gable with an attached projecting corner turret, built to enhance the dramatic effect of the castle. Behind the single-foil windows and the three lancet windows above is the great hall.

NEO–GOTHIC
18th to 19th c.

The renewed interest in Gothic architecture which begun in the 18th century can partly be attributed to Gothic novels and other scholarly works, especially the writings of the architect Viollet-le-Duc (1814-1879). Gradually the revival of Gothic had overtaken the alternative Neo-classical style to become the dominant style in the new grandiose architectural projects in Europe, Canada and to a lesser degree in the USA. The British government has chosen to rebuilt the Houses of Parliament in London (1839-1888), in the Neo-Gothic style to emphasize national pride in its past. In Germany and Austria castles of the period adorn romantic mountainsides and assert their national identities by evoking an exotic aspect of the Nordic tradition of the owner as a mythical hero – that could only be expressed through Gothic Revival with its high-pitched roofs, tall towers, turrets, dormers and gables.

The undulating curve of the 'Karahafu' gable with broad overhang at the Himeji Castle, 1601–13, Japan.

Shibi, A Japanese ornamental tile set on both ends of the ridgepole that tops the shingled roof. Many such ornaments, anthropomorphic or animal, adorn the foof tops of traditional buildings in Japan. Osaka Castle, Japan.

Osaka Castle, built in 1583 and restored in 1997, Japan. All castles have traditional pagoda-like roof forms and highly decorated gables.

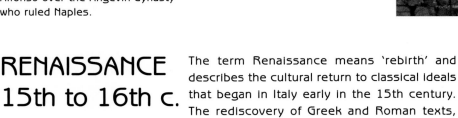

Castel Nuovo, 13th c. Naples, Italy. Renaissance entrance – Arch of Alfonso d'Aragona, 1455–1466. This triumphal arch was erected to commemorate the victory of King Alfonso over the Angevin dynasty who ruled Naples.

RENAISSANCE 15th to 16th c.

The term Renaissance means 'rebirth' and describes the cultural return to classical ideals that began in Italy early in the 15th century. The rediscovery of Greek and Roman texts, statuary and architecture brought about a revival for harmony, clarity and strength. These characteristics soon spread to many European countries. The elegance, though, of Renaissance architecture is less suited to the needs of military fortification. Therefore, the term Renaissance is specific only to those parts of a castle that have classical elements incorporated in their construction. Doorways and widows with pediments, columns of the classical order or other Renaissance features, are usually found on residential or religious buildings facing the inner courtyard or bailey of the castle and were built during the 15th or 16th centuries.

Castles in JAPAN 15th to 17th c.

At a time when building Castles as strongholds in Europe declined, political instability in Japan in the 16th and early 17th centuries, necessitated an increase of Castle building for military use. Massive stone fortifications were built at the base level of towers, (due to the introduction of fire-arms from Europe in the mid-16th century), with structures of wood built above it. Thickly plastered outer walls reduced the risk of fire. An inventive earthquake-resistant technique was devised by the Japanese to hold these tall wooden towers, with the use of a massive tree trunk passing through the normally five-story structures, locking the whole framework together. The upper floors served as quarters for the lords, command centers and watchtowers. Many courtyards within the curtain walls kept the main tower safe from attack.

The thirteenth-century Great Hall in Chillon Castle, Switzerland.

Slit or Loophole

Crenellations

Machicolated parapet, or gallery

Corbel (brackets)

Turret, a small observation tower, containing a stairway

The private rooms of the Lord's family

Holes supporting the beams of the scaffolding during construction

Window of the Great Hall

Garderobe. High up in the tower a shaft within the thickness of the wall served as a toilet

Lord's Kitchen

Chapel

Chapel at Dover Castle, c1180, England. A small, but a fine example of the late Norman style.

Household Dormitories and Hall

Crenellations on the battlements of the curtain wall

The GREAT TOWER of the Castilo de la Mota, 1440–1480. Spain. The location of rooms as annotated, is in keeping with that of most Keeps, although the layout inside this one may differ a little.

MACHICOLATIONS,
In late Medieval times towers and gateways had gaps, called machicolations, between the corbels that supported the projected crenellated parapets. Machicolations allowed archers to observe and defend the vulnerable base of the castle.

A view of a Great Hall. Food was prepaired behind screens at the far end.

Re-enactment of kitchen activities at Sterling Castle, Scotland.

The GREAT TOWER, also referred to as KEEP or DONJON, is the most secure of all the buildings in the castle complex and obviously the most important. The layout comprises of three main areas: the lord's private apartments at the very top; the lofty Great Hall, in the middle, occupied two-thirds of the interior space of the tower; and, the household rooms near the ground level where the water well and store rooms were also to be found. The prison or dungeon was often below ground level. The Great Tower was surrounded by a walled enclosure forming a Bailey in which barracks, workshops and stables were located.

Underground prison at Chillon Castle, Switzerland.

PRISONS and DUNGEONS
In medieval times most captives were either political or state prisoners and were held in special chambers or in one of the towers in modest comfort. There are, however, a few grim undercroft cells and the sinister 'Bottle Dungeons' – dark and underground and entered through a narrow hatch on the floor above. Ordinary criminals were not imprisoned, but punished severely or executed.

KITCHENS
In early castles the kitchens were detached from the tower or other castle buildings. Later on when the lord's kitchen was moved next to the Great Hall, the kitchen was provided with a stone vault and isolated by a substantial wall to avoid the risk of fire. The servants' kitchen was usually close to their living chambers.

ALHAMBRA: Dome of the Hall of the Abencerrajes.
The little plaster vaults known as *muqarnas* ('honeycombed' work) and other decorative Arabesque elements have no structural function, but are purely ornamental according to a systematic geometrical arrangement. The effect is mesmerizing.

BELOW: The richly decorated arches of one of the projecting pavilions in the Courtyard of the Lions are supported on slender columns. 1354–1391. Alhambra, Granada, Andalusia, Spain.

Moorish decoration, known as Arabesque, demonstrates the fascination and preoccupation, of the Islamic artists with the dynamic process of generating intricate patterns through repetition and symmetry. Alhambra, Granada, Andalusia, Spain.

ISLAM 8th to 15th c. & MOORISH Spain

The Islamic world within a century after its foundation in AD 622 stretched from the borders of India to Spain. Invading forces who settled in North Africa and Spain are given the name 'Moors' (from the Greek *mauros* meaning 'dark'). 'Moorish' refers to the architectural style that emerged from the fusion that took place between the various national stylistic traditions. At Granada, in Andalusia, Spain, between the 13th and 15th centuries a citadel was built with quadrangular towers. The two palaces of the Alhambra lay within the fortified walls. The large halls, the banqueting room, state rooms and private apartments are in the distinctive moorish architectural style of decoration – carved stucco, tiles and mosaic with Arabesque geometric designs, interlacing representations of plants and scripts from proverbs and passages from the Koran.

Introduction

One of the earliest defensive instincts of settled man was to barricade himself against attackers. From palisades of thorn bushes to masonry walls, the art of fortification developed apace with social, political and technological advancement. Castles are normally associated with the feudal order of society in Europe during the Middle Ages, that stretched broadly between the ninth and the 15th centuries. A system of military vassalage led to the development of innumerable fortified knightly strongholds, that varied considerably in size, strength and style of construction. Castles dominated the countryside in Europe, and also in the Levant and Asia. The essential elements of castle architecture developed in each region at varying times, and new techniques often traveled from one place to another in the baggage train of medieval armies and kings.

Milecastle 39 on Hadrian's Wall, an ancient Roman fortification in Engalnd.

ANCIENT TOWN WALLS

The forerunners of castles were the town walls of ancient cities in Sumeria, Greece, Mesopotamia and Egypt. Though in ruins now, archaeological evidence and literary references point to them being fairly extensive and well-planned structures, with towers and imposing gateways. The system of communal defenses continued till Roman times ,when impressive fortified cities and military outposts were built all over the far-flung empire. Hadrian's Wall in England (c.130 CE) is an example of the standardized Roman military fortification. It was 75 miles (120 km) long, punctuated with castles at every mile (milecastles), and 160 turrets. The formidable walls of Constantinople, capital of the Eastern Roman empire (or Byzantine Empire) were considered unassailable in the ancient world.

The Anglo-Saxons and Vikings enclosed settlements with earth and wood fortifications, and these were common in England, western Europe and the Slavic lands until the 10th century, and even later in eastern Europe.

A restored section of the ancient walls of Constantinople.

THE AGE OF CASTLES

The 10th century heralded the 'Age of Castles' in Europe. The feudal system of decentralized authority based on a system of granting fiefs in lieu of military service became the order of the day, and a knight's castle became a mark of status. Kings, princes, nobles and knights lived and ruled from their fortified residences. Soldiers and their horses were quartered within its walls, as was the bailiff, the armorer, the priest, the knight's family and a multitude of retainers. The stores had weapons, grain and supplies, if necessary, to withstand a long siege, and there was usually space in the castle grounds to accommodate villagers and townspeople in times of war. There was also a prison, either in a tower or perhaps a dank dungeon, and many castles continued as prisons long after they outlived their administrative and residential roles. Usually, they controlled a radius of 10-15 miles (15–25 km), which was the area patrolled by the resident garrison.

Bodiam Castle in England has a towered bailey, sited in a deep moat.

Castles could be part of fortified towns, called *bastides* in France, or they could be standing by themselves in a naturally defended spot, such as on ridge or hill, or by a cliff or a river. Sometimes they were sited in a man-made moat or a raised platform. They occurred singly, or as a string of defensive structures along a contentious border.

The Gothic age (13th–15th century) was the main era of castle building in Europe. Stone castles dominated in northern and western Europe, the Middle-east and parts of Asia, while brick structures were common in the Iberian Peninsula, and in low-lying areas in the north. Stone became common in construction after 1250 in eastern Europe. Timber was used everywhere for flooring, roofs, beams and scaffolding. Spanish castles built after the Reconquista have a strong Moorish element in castle design, and are marvels of brickwork. The Renaissance brought in more ornate decoration in the roofs and interiors, and castles veered towards palaces in comfort and luxury. The advent of artillery led to changes in the design, and the defensive role of castles gradually decreased after the 15th century.

By the 16th century, castles evolved into ornate, romantic structures that resembled palaces rather than fortified strongholds. In the 19th century, there was a revival of interest in many of the medieval citadels that had been abandoned and left to ruin. These were now seen as remnants of a chivalric, more honorable age. Restoration efforts began to gain currency, and at present, many castles are protected monuments, and have been converted to museums.

ADVENT OF GUNPOWDER

Artillery became commonplace by the middle of the 14th century, and castles were adapted with new gunports to allow small artillery fire. Often, lower bulwarks were built in front of existing walls to provide a suitable platform for artillery weapons. Cannons replaced the trebuchet as the favored attack weapon from the 15th century. Angled walls were more vulnerable to cannon fire than rounded towers. Soon, permanant artillery fortifications became the main line of defence,and it was apparent that the age of traditional medieval warfare was ending.

ELEMENTS OF A CASTLE

The art of military architecture developed gradually over time, with many regional variations in the defensive elements, architectural styles and material used.

Motte and Bailey The classic castle form was the Norman motte and bailey. This consisted of a raised earthen mound called motte, enclosed by a timber palisade and surmounted by a tower called the donjon. A deep ditch ran around the motte, and its enclosed yard was called the bailey. Over time, a second palisade enclosed a second bailey, surrounded by another ditch or water-filled moat. Gateways with drawbridges restricted entry, and a platform ran along the inner edge of the wall, called the wall walk or the *chemin de ronde*.

The keep or donjon, Tower Houses Between the 10th and the 11th centuries, wooden structures gave way to stone. The donjons, known later as keeps, grew in size to several floors, containing the main halls, chapel, and stores. Initially square, they developed into rectangular, round and octagonal structures. Some of them were massive, self-contained structures, such as Orford in England, and Loches in France.

The keep could be standing independently, or placed against the curtain wall in the most secure part of the bailey or the castle ward. By the end of the 12th century, castles grew into several baileys defended by towered and turreted walls. Usually the inner bailey was at one side, backed up against the cliff or the river for greater protection. As keeps became heavier and better defended, the motte reduced in height and was eventually eliminated.

After the 13th century, large Tower Houses became the fashion. One or more of the corner towers was enlarged into several vaulted floors, with the main residential and administrative chambers. These were in the most secure part of the bailey, and were the last resort of the defenders in case the walls were overrun by attackers. In Germany, tall tower houses were called *bergfried*, and the Spanish variant was the imposing Torre del Homenaje (or Homage Tower)

Walls and Towers Castle walls grew in complexity with the use of masonry. There could be an inner or outer wall, the former much higher than the latter. In larger castles, there was a third enclosure, or the outer curtain joined to the town walls to create a fortified town or *bastide*.

Towers could be placed at the corners, as well as at intervals along the perimeter. Mural towers were part of the wall, while flanking towers projected out to provide flanking fire at the base of the walls. Towers could be round, square, D-shaped, or polygonal. Open-backed towers contained wooden fighting platforms for soldiers. Covered or open wall walks connected the towers for easy movement of supplies and men. Conversely, it also provided attackers with easy access to all parts of the castle once a section of the wall was breached.

Castles were rebuilt often, and the height and thickness of walls and towers varied with each new phase. From the 12th century, castle builders incorporated many elements from forts in the Levant, such as battered sloping plinths, and the concentric arrangement of regularly spaced walls and towers.

Battlements These followed the perimeter of the walls and towers, and there were various kinds of merlons and embrasures. During the 12th century, both the castle walls and towers had provision for overhanging wooden fighting platforms to be erected in times of war. The floors of the hoardings had gaps from which projectiles could be hurled at attackers attempting to undermine or climb the walls. These hoardings were vulnerable to fire, and gradually replaced with corbeled stone platforms called machicolations.

Arrow loops in the walls also took many shapes, depending on the weapons to be used, such as bows, crossbows, hand guns and artillery.

Gatehouses and Barbicans A strong gatehouse was critical to the survival of the castle. The entry point was usually guarded by twin towers with a barbican or forework, one or several drawbridges, and a wood-iron portcullis. The narrow passage between the gate towers would contain murder holes or *meurtrieres* in the ceiling, from which the defenders would drop boiling oil or pitch on unwelcome visitors. Along the sides would be arrow loops for archers to attack from concealed passages in the walls. Sometimes, the gatehouse was a fortress in itself, and contained the castellan's residence.

The Moat One of the oldest features of fortified strongholds, it varied from a simple trench to a large, water-filled ditch, with sharpened stakes at the bottom. Moats could be single or multiple, and joined with other barriers such as a cliffside or the sea or river.

Facing page:
The spectacular Torre del Homenaje at Segovia Castle in Spain, with corbeled corner turrets called bartizans.

The 11th-century Cardiff Castle in Wales has a Norman keep and curtain wall, placed on a man-made motte.

The unusually high 14th-century donjon at the Château de Vincennes, France. It is sited in a large bailey, with corner turrets and a covered wall walk.

The bridge across the moat leading to a a twin-towered gateway at the fortified town of Carcassonne, France. Note the wooden hoardings along the wall and the round tower.

CASTLE CONSTRUCTION

The first step in building a castle was to choose a site, preferably with good natural defenses such as a cliff, a river bank, an island, or a peninsula. Most castles are placed on the highest elevation in the area, overlooking the settlement below, and with a clear view of the surrounding countryside. Rocky hilltops provided the best foundation, as enemy miners would have a hard time tunneling through the rock base. Access to a river provided water for the moat, and ensured a supply line in times of crisis.

Construction was laborious and expensive. An average castle could take anywhere between five to ten years to raise. Upwards of 2000 men, under the supervision of master masons, were involved in building the bigger castles. Among those employed were quarriers, woodcutters, hammerers, diggers, mortar makers, lime-burners, smiths, plasterers, glass-makers and carters. Some of the master masons were highly regarded, such as Bishop Gandulph of Rochester (11th century), Master James of St George (1230–1309), and the da Sangallo family of architects in Italy (15th century). Not many records of accounts have survived, but there is evidence that Edward I spent thousands of pounds on his Welsh castles. By contrast, only £100 was allotted by King John for the curtain wall at Carrickfergus in the early 13th century.

Limestone was favored in England and France, and brought to the site by wagon or boat. The stone obtained from digging the moat was commonly used as rubble to fill in the gaps between the two layers of dressed stone. Timber came from surrounding forests. Glass was a precious commodity and used sparingly.

SEIGE WARFARE

Almost as much thought was expended on the means to bring down a castle as to raise it. There were various steps involved in taking a castle.

The first was to cross the moat. This was achieved by sliding planks across the gap (if it was narrow) or by draining it and filling it with mud, rocks and branches in case of a wider ditch. All this was done under a rain of arrows and fiery projectiles sent by the defenders at the battlements.

The next step was to breach the walls and gate. This required the use of a battering ram, which was usually an iron-tipped log of wood mounted on a carriage. Mobile shelters of wet hides called 'cats' covered the ram, and were also used by miners and sappers working at the base of the towers and walls. Their job was to tunnel deep under the structure, and engineer a fire or an explosion to trigger its collapse.

Attempts to scale the wall with ladders were fraught with danger, and required strong covering fire by archers, or better still, a distraction on another part of the wall. The best way was to roll a wooden tower on wheels to the curtain, and lower a drawbridge to the battlements. These siege towers had several levels for archers, crossbowmen and foot soldiers. Getting them to the walls was a feat in itself, but once placed, they were usually very effective.

Once onto the wall walk, the attackers worked swiftly to take control of the key areas of the castle, such as the keep and main towers, as well as the gatehouse. Sometimes only a portion of the castle was won, and the forces regrouped for the next round of action.

Many of the weapons used in the middle ages go back to antiquity, such as giant crossbows, and catapults (mangonels) that hurled stones. Crossbowmen and archers used mobile wooden shields or mantlets to get close enough to shoot at the walls. Trebuchets became popular in the 13th century, and could hurl stones weighing upto 300 lbs (150 kg).

It was also a waiting game, as eventually the castle would run out of food, ammunition and men. With so many wounded and dying, there was also the ever present danger of disease. Though many castles had their own wells, the attackers would do their best to disrupt or contaminate the castle's water supply.

MASTER JAMES OF ST GEORGE
A noted military engineer of his time, Jacques de Saint-Georges d'Espéranche hailed from a family of master masons in Savoy. He came to England in the late 1270s at the behest of Edward I, and designed many of his Welsh castles including Harlech, Conwy, Caernarfon and Beaumaris. Master James perfected the design of the concentric castle, with levels of strategic defensive elements. He was appointed Master of the Royal Works in Wales in 1285, at the princely salary of three shilling a day. In 1290, he was appointed Constable of Harlech Castle.

An illustration of a siege engine at work.

A 15th century illustration of a castle siege during the 100 Years' War (1337-1453).

GREEK FIRE
Invented in the Byzantine empire, this was an incendiary weapon used effecively in naval warfare, as well as in castle defense. The formula for the liquid has been lost in time, but it was projected at the enemy through specially designed siphons. This is probably one of the earliest uses of chemical weapons. Hot pitch, water and oil were also poured down from the battlements, and even animal and human urine (as an effective flame retardent).

Facing page: The alpine hill castle at Tarasp in Switzerland.

The 12th century Crusader castle in Syria, Krak des Chevaliers, is a perfect example of a concentric castle.

A vaulted interior room in a structure at Rhodes Castle, Greece.

Arrow slit in the wall at the !3th century Fort La Latte in France.

The barbican and gateway at the 11th century Lewes Castle, England. Note the arrow slits, and the machicolations over the entrance.

Murder holes, or meurtrières, at Bodiam Castle, England.

Wall walk at Castello de Sao Jorges in Lisbon, Portugal.
Facing page: The 13th-century Norman castle at Limerick in Ireland, on the banks of the Shannon River.

Pyramidal spurs strengthen the curtain wall at the 12th century Goodrich Castle, England.

Fine brickwork at Malbork Castle in Poland.

Vienna

Salzburg

AUSTRIA

Hohensalzburg Castle

One of the largest medieval castles in Europe, Hohensalzburg straddles a high ridge called Festungsberg hill, above the picturesque town of Salzburg. It was one among several strongholds built by the influential Archbishop Gebhard von Helfenstein, of the sovereign Bishopric of Salzburg, in the late 11th century. From a simple wooden fortification the castle gradually expanded to include stone walls, towers, and domestic ranges. It was considerably extended and lavishly decorated by Bishop Leonhard von Keutschach, who lived in the castle in the early part of the 15th century. At this time there was large scale unrest in Europe to protest against church levies and taxes. During the Peasants War of 1525, Hohensalzburg was besieged by a violent mob of farmers and townspeople. Salzburg was annexed by Austria in 1805, after which the castle was used as a warehouse and military barracks till 1861. It served as a detention center until the end of World War II.

The architecture is a mix of various styles, ranging from sturdy Romanesque exteriors to elaborate Gothic interiors. The Golden Room has red marble spiral columns, beautifully carved and gilded paneling and a superbly tiled late Gothic stove.

ADDRESS	Fortress Mönchsberg 34, 5020 Salzburg, Austria
CONSTRUCTION HISTORY	**1077** First castle, probably wooden
	14th–15th century Walls, round towers and residential apartments; granary
	1510 Golden Room and Great Hall
	16th–17th century Outer gun bastions
COMMISSIONED BY	Bishops of Salzburg
MATERIALS	Stone, timber
STYLE	Rock castle; Romanesque

A short 10-minute ride on the funicular railway connects the city center below with the castle. Salzburg is famous as the birthplace of Mozart, and the castle hosts the widely acclaimed Salzburg Fortress Music Concerts. Several medieval festivals and markets are also included in the annual events calendar, including the immensely popular St George's Cavalcade on 25 April. The Fortress Museum is also housed within the castle.

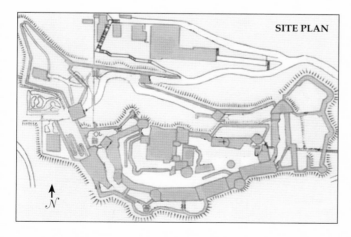

SITE PLAN

N

Facing page:
The white-walled fortress of Hohensalzburg overlooks the charming town of Salzburg, better known as the birthplace of the composer Mozart.

The exterior façade of the castle chapel.

An intricately decorated ceiling.

Gravensteen
• Brussels

BELGIUM

Gravensteen Castle

Gravensteen or the 'Castle of the Counts' is situated at the confluence of the rivers Lieve and Lys at Ghent. The earliest structure here was a timber fort built as a defense against the Vikings. This was followed by a stone structure around 1000 CE, traces of which can still be seen in the foundations of the present castle built by Philip of Alsace, on his return from the Crusades in 1180. Under his direction, Gravensteen grew into a formidable fortress, and it was the main residence and administrative headquarters of the counts in the ensuing centuries. It was twice besieged by the burghers of Ghent in 1301 and 1338, and the Prince's Court of Justice was housed in the castle between 1407–1708. After the Counts moved out to a more comfortable mansion in the city, Gravensteen continued to function as a mint, a prison, and then finally a cotton mill in the 19th century, when workers' quarters were set up along the bailey wall.

The design of Gravensteen was inspired by the Crusader castles in the Levant. An outer curtain wall encloses a keep containing the vaulted chambers of the Great Hall, with attached kitchens and the castellan's quarters. The Count's residence was a separate building behind the keep. The curtain wall has 24 semi-circular turrets, called bartizans, supported by wall buttresses. These were open backed structures with arrow loops below and embrasures secured by wooden shutters above. An extended gatehouse and barbican led to the main doorway. This was protected by a *bretèche*, or an overhead stone machicolation. A cross-shaped window in the entrance hall proclaimed it to be the residence of a Crusader knight.

The imposing front façade of this notable water castle.

ADDRESS	Sint-Veerleplein, Ghent, Belgium
CONSTRUCTION HISTORY	**Ninth century** Timber fort
	1000 First stone buildings
	1180s Donjon, curtain wall with bartizans and extended barbican gateway, Count's palace
	14th century Additions and repairs after repeated sieges
COMMISSIONED BY	Philip of Alsace, Count of Flanders
MATERIALS	Timber, stone
STYLE	Water castle, bailey, tower keep

In 1885, Gravensteen was purchased by the city of Ghent and has since been painstakingly restored. The castle exhibits a fascinating collection of medieval arms and armor, as well as a collection of medieval torture instruments.

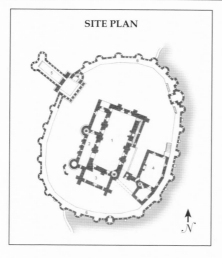

SITE PLAN

The wall walk all along the battlements.

Facing page:
Designed by a crusader count, Gravensteen was an important administrative center. The semi-circular turrets along the wall are supported by wall buttresses.

Brussels
Beersel
BELGIUM

Beersel Castle

A strategic castle in the defense of Brussels, Beersel is a brick and stone fortification positioned at the center of a lake. It is an example of a water castle, raised by Godfrey of Hallebeek, who was Seneschal to the Duke of Brabant. Beersel was damaged during the wars of succession of Brabant (1356–57), and again in 1491 during the Revolt of the Towns, when a civil war broke out between the nobles of the region and Maxmilian of Austria. The lord of Beersel, Henrik III, aroused the ire of the townspeople by supporting Maxmilian, and they besieged the Castle with heavy artillery. Though the garrison surrendered, Maxmilian eventually retook the Castle, and thereafter added considerably to its defenses.

Instead of a main donjon, there are three horseshoe-shaped towers attached to the curtain wall, designed to resist artillery. These contained the garrison quarters and lords' chambers, as well as the other functional rooms. Loopholes and machicolations lined the upper perimeter of the towers and walls. Tiled roofs were added in the 17th century, with the distinctive Flemish stepped gables.

ADDRESS	Beersel, Flemish Brabant, Flanders, Belgium
CONSTRUCTION HISTORY	**13th century** First stone structure
	1300–10 Walled enclosure within a broad moat
	1491 Three horseshoe-shaped towers
	1930s Restoration begun
COMMISSIONED BY	Godfrey of Hallebeke
MATERIALS	Brick (curtain wall), sandstone and timber (towers)
STYLE	Water castle

The castle has been uninhabited since the 18th century. For a brief while, it was occupied by a cotton factory, and in 1928, it was donated to the League of Friends of Beersel Castle, which began the process of restoration.

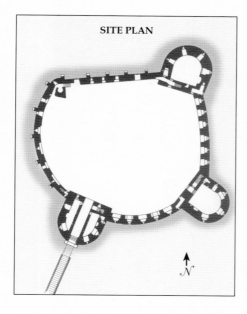

SITE PLAN

N

The stepped gables of the red brick Castle's tower are reminiscent of Flemish architecture.

A bridge across the water leads to the main entrance of the castle.

Facing page:
The three towers at Beersel look into a circular castle yard. A covered wall walk.connects the towers.

CANADA

Laurier Castle
Ottawa

Laurier Castle

Located in the heart of the city next to the Rideau Canal, the Château Laurier is an impressive historic landmark of Ottawa. It was commissioned in 1909 by Charles Melville Hays, the chairman of the Grand Trunk Railway of Canada, who also built the adjacent Union Station. Despite some disagreements with the architects, the construction of this spectacular palace-like hotel was completed in 1912. Unfortunately, while traveling to the inauguration, Sir Charles Hays perished aboard the *Titanic* on 15 April, 1912. The Château Laurier was eventually opened by its namesake, Sir Wilfrid Laurier, a former Prime Minister of Canada, on 12 June, 1912. Sir Charles' ghost is said to haunt the hotel looking for the ceremony that he missed, a fact that adds considerably to the hotel's allure.

Ownership passed to the Canadian National Railway in 1922, and then to the Canadian National Hotels. From its inception, the hotel has attracted the wealthy and the famous from around the world, as well as royalty and heads of state and government. Prime Minister RB Bennet lived in a suite during his term in office from 1930–35. It is the obvious meeting place for politicians, as Parliament Hill is just a stone's throw away, so much so that the château is sometimes referred to as the 'third chamber of Parliament'. The Canadian Broadcasting Corporation had the offices of its English and French radio stations at the hotel during 1924–2004.

The hotel was designed to replicate a late Renaissance château in France, and the elegant façade and opulent interiors more that fulfill that intention. The building base consists of granite blocks, on which rests the superstructure of limestone, capped with copper roofing. The interiors are resplendent with marble floors, brass fittings and valuable antiques.

ADDRESS	1 Rideau Street, Ottawa, Canada
CONSTRUCTION HISTORY	1907–12
COMMISSIONED BY	Charles Melville Hays, President of the Grand Trunk Railway of Canada
ARCHITECTS	Bradford Gilbert, Ross and Macfarlane
MATERIALS	Limestone
STYLE	Palace- castle; Canadian railway hotel

The Château Laurier is presently owned and managed by Fairmont Hotels and Resorts.

The attractive lines of the château are reminiscent of French Renaissance architecture.

Above: An aerial view of Ottawa with the Château Laurier in the foreground.
Facing page: Château Laurier is located in the heart of city, next to the Rideau Canal, and close to the Union Station.

An elegantly capped corner turret.

CANADA

Frontenec •
Ottawa

Frontenec Castle

The Canadian Pacific Railway company built several luxury hotels in Canada in the late 19th and early 20th century, in a successful effort to encourage train travel, and build up a wealthy clientele. One of these establishments was the splendid Château Frontenac, located on a high promontory in the heart of the city of Quebec, with splendid views across the St Lawrence River. It was commissioned in the late 19th century by William van Horne, the general manager of the Canadian Pacific Railway. It is named for Loius de Baude, Count of Frontenac, who was the far-sighted governor of New France during 1672–98. His coat of arms is placed at the entrance arch.

The château opened its doors in 1893, and since then has been a landmark hotel of the city. The guests have included in their number royal personages, heads of state, politicians, film stars and barons of industry, such as George VI, Charles de Gaulle, Chiang-Kai Shek, Princess Grace of Monaco, Francois Mitterrand, and Alfred Hitchcock. The Quebec Conference of 1943 attended by Franklin D Roosevelt and Winston Churchill took place at the Frontenac.

The architect Bruce Price built the château in the best tradition of European extravagance, in a design style derived from the late Renaissance period. The Claude-Pratte Wing includes an indoor pool and an outdoor terrace. The hotel has 618 elegantly furnished rooms and suites.

ADDRESS	Château Frontenac, Quebec city Canada
CONSTRUCTION HISTORY	**1893** Construction complete
	1993 Claude-Pratte wing
COMMISSIONED BY	William van Horne of the Canadian Pacific Railway
ARCHITECT	Bruce Price
MATERIALS	Stone
STYLE	Palace-castle; Canadian railway hotel

At present, the hotel is managed by Fairmont Hotels and Resorts, and owned by Legacy Hotels REIT.

The hotel is illuminated in the evening.

Facing page:
Château Frontenac was one among a chain of luxurious railway hotels in Canada, that was intended to attract wealthy sections of society to the charms of train travel.

Detail of the façade.

Prague

CZECH REPUBLIC

Hukvaldy

Hukvaldy Castle

Surrounded by the thick forests of a game preserve in Ostravia, the elongated Gothic structure of Hukvaldy Castle is one of the strongest fortifications in the Czech Republic. It was first built in the 13th century by the German born Counts of Hückeswagen, who were granted the estate by the Czech king Premsyl Otakar I. The lands were subsequently given to the Bishop of Olumouc in 1359, after which Hukvaldy became the center of a valuable archdiocese. The castle changed hands several times during periods of financial crisis and political uncertainty. It was briefly held by King Sigismund of Hungary, then by the Hussite commander Jan Capek, and also for a time by the Czech king Jiri of Podebrady. It eventually reverted back to the Olumouc archdiocese that held it until its nationalization in 1948. The castle was reduced to a ruin, and abandoned after a devastating fire in 1762. The most famous resident of Hukvaldy was the 19th-century composer Leoš Janáček, whose opera *The Cunning Little Vixen* was inspired by the romantic environs of Hukvaldy Castle.

The Gothic Knight's all and chapel date to the mid-13th century, and form part of the oldest section of the castle. Additional floors and quarters were added from the 15th century onwards. Strong artillery bastions were constructed in the 16th century, and the Baroque St Andrew's Chapel dates to the 17th century. The coat of arms of various Olumouc bishops can be seen over the castle gates.

ADDRESS	739 46 Hukvaldy, Frýdek-Místek county, Czech Republic
CONSTRUCTION HISTORY	**15th century** White Tower
	16th century Expansion with round artillery bastions; red deer parks established
	17th century St Andrew's Chapel
	1762 Destroyed in fire
COMMISSIONED BY	Counts of Hückeswagen
MATERIALS	Stone and timber
STYLE	Rock castle; Gothic

The castle estate is a nature heritage site, with many species of local fauna. Since 1993, the town hosts the Janáček's Hukvaldy International Music Festival in June and July each year, when concerts are held in the castle grounds and in St Andrew's Chapel. There is a bronze statue of the 'Cunning Little Vixen' in the castle park. Touching its tail is believed to bring good luck.

The castle entranceway.

The bronze statue of the 'Cunning Little Vixen' in the castle estate.

Facing page:
A battlemented wall connects the two ends of Hukvaldy castle, which is located atop a ridge in a thickly forested game reserve in the region of Moravia-Silesia. St Andrew's Chapel can be seen in the center along the wall.

Karlštejn • Prague
CZECH REPUBLIC

Karlštejn Hrad

Karlštejn Castle in Bohemia is the most well-preserved castle in the Czech Republic. It was commissioned in 1348 by the king of Bohemia, Charles IV (also the Holy Roman Emperor), as a summer retreat, and a secure repository for sacred relics and the coronation jewels of the empire. It was especially chosen for its remote location amid dense forests just 16 miles (25 km) southwest of the capital at Prague. The Emperor supervised much of the construction which was completed by 1365, when the Chapel of the Holy Cross was consecrated. During the terrible Hussite Wars of the 15th century, the Czech crown jewels were also moved for safekeeping to Karlštejn.

The castle was originally built in the Gothic style, but later renovations added a Renaissance touch to the interiors, particularly in the painted walls of the imperial chambers. An interesting feature is the wooden hoardings at the top of the towers, which served as machicolations in times of attack. In the late 19th century, the exterior façade of the castle was restored in a neo-Gothic style by the architect Josef Mocker.

There are several tall towers in the castle, which increase in importance from the Well Tower at the lowest level to the Great Tower at the highest point. The Burgraves Palace near the entrance was the residence of the castellan, which was followed by the five-storied Imperial Palace. Adjacent to this is the Marian Tower with the collegiate church of St Catherine. Last of all is the Great Tower which rises to a height of 200 ft (60 m). The Chapel of the Holy Rood located within the tower is decorated with 129 panel paintings of saints and Czech kings, some of which are the work of the outstanding medieval painter, Theodoric of Prague. Precious gems are studded in the walls, and the Chapel is said to contain a piece of the True Cross.

ADDRESS	Státní hrad Karlštejn, 267 18 Karlštejn, Czech Republic
CONSTRUCTION HISTORY	**1348** Construction begins
	1365 Consecration of the Chapel of the Holy Rood
	15–16th century Additions and reconstruction
	Late 19th century Restoration of exteriors
COMMISSIONED BY	Charles IV, Holy Roman Emperor
MATERIALS	Stone, timber, brick
STYLE	Rock castle; Gothic, Renaissance

Among the crown jewels on display is a replica of the crown of St Wenceslas, a 10th century martyred prince who was canonized after his death. He is the patron saint of the Czech people.

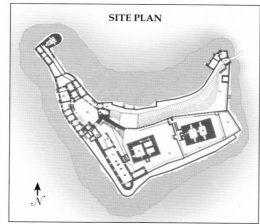

SITE PLAN

N

The coronation jewels of the Holy Roman Empire were kept in the Great Tower.

Details of the brick work in the interior buildings.

Facing page:
The walls of Karlstejn Hrad rise out of the rock face.
The exterior façade has been fully restored.

Křivoklát
Prague
CZECH REPUBLIC

Křivoklát Hrad

Křivoklát Castle was a prominent hunting castle of the Přemyslid dynasty that ruled Bohemia and Hungary in the 13th century. Construction of the hrad was begun by Přemysl Otakar II (*r.* 1253–78) and finished by his successor, Václav II. It is located in the densely forested valley of Rakovnicky just 30 miles (48 km) west of Prague. Rebuilt by Wladislaw Jagiello in the late 15th century, Křivoklát was converted to a dreaded prison in the 17th century. It was extensively restored by the Fürstenberg family in the 19th and 20th centuries.

Built on triangular plan, Křivoklát is a dense complex of structures in the best tradition of Czech castle architecture. The prominent Huderka Tower offers splendid views of the countryside. The interiors display a valuable collection of Gothic panel paintings and there is a permanent exposition of hunting weapons. The Fürstenberg Library is impressive, as is the castle chapel and the late Gothic hall.

ADDRESS	Státní hrad Křivoklát, 270 23 Křivoklát, Czech Republic
CONSTRUCTION HISTORY	**13th century** Original castle
	15th century Rebuilt
	1643 Burned down
	19–20th century Restoration and conversion to museum
COMMISSIONED BY	Přemysl Otakar II of Bohemia
MATERIALS	Stone, timber
STYLE	Rock castle

The castle jail and torture chamber are also part of the museum, as is the large castle kitchen.

The passage going up to the inner castle.

SITE PLAN

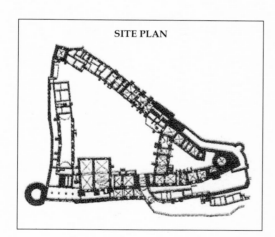

A royal Coat of Arms.

Facing page:
Krivoklát Castle in Bohemia was originally a royal hunting lodge.

Prague
•
CZECH REPUBLIC
•
Pernštejn

Pernštejn Castle

This formidable medieval castle in Moravia was the seat of the ambitious Pernštejn family that ruled this region as an autonomous fief through much of the Middle Ages. The castle was founded towards the end of the 13th century by the first recorded ancestor of the family, Stephen of Medlov, who was granted large tracts in the Moravian uplands. The family grew in influence and fortune during the political turmoil of the next centuries, and the impressive Pernštejn Castle reflected their growing power. The family declined in influence towards the end of the 16th century, and the property changed hands many times. At present it is owned by the state.

The architecture covers a range of styles, from Gothic and Renaissance to Rococo. The rock castle is naturally protected on three sides by a steep slope, and several gatehouses, moats and bastions added several more layers of man-made defense. A marble-like white stone was used in the exterior façade to give Pernštejn an unusually shining appearance. There are five towers, all on different levels, and the main tower has projecting turrets with machicolations, akin to bartizans. The entrance hall is decorated with alveolar vaulting, and the interior spaces in the castle have carefully preserved stucco work and fresco paintings from the 17th and 18th century.

ADDRESS	Státní hrad Pernštejn, 592 62 Nedvědice
CONSTRUCTION HISTORY	**13th century** Original five-story castle tower and wall
	1450s Damaged by fire
	15th–16th century Extensive building—residential towers, chapels, gatehouses, bastions and moats.
	17th–19th century Baroque renovations in the rooms.
	1716 Franz Eckstein decorated the ceilings of the chapel; stucco work in Knights Hall
COMMISSIONED BY	The lords of Pernštejn
MATERIALS	Stone, timber, plaster
STYLE	Rock castle; Gothic, Renaissance

A stunning location and the fascinating maze of buildings in the interior have made Pernštejn one of the most visited castles in the country.

Facing page:
A maze of tall structures on different levels, this Moravian castle was the stronghold of the Pernštejn family for 300 years.

Detail of the unusual corbeling at the windows.

The castle entranceway.

ENGLAND
Orford
London

Orford Castle

The young Plantagenet king, Henry II (*r.* 1154-89), ordered the construction of Orford castle in an effort to contain the growing power of Hugh Bigod, the influential Earl of Norfolk, who was located at nearby Framlingham castle. Public records of the time show that £1413 was spent on the construction of the donjon which included draining the surrounding marsh to create a safe harbor.

Orford is a unique variation of the Norman castle design. A spacious central keep, rising 90 ft (27 m) high is circular from the inside, but externally polygonal with 21 facets. This was probably done to avoid the blind spots for archers inherent in structures with right-angled corners. The keep consists of a basement and two upper floors, and a forebuilding leads into the main entranceway, above which is the chapel. Tower staircases and numerous passages connect together a maze of living quarters on several levels. There is also a kitchen, and a well located in the basement. The external walls rise high to mask the roof. A curtain wall, towers and gatehouse completed the complex but they have long since disappeared.

The castle was heavily garrisoned in 1177 during the revolt of Henry the Young King, elder son of Henry II. It was briefly captured by the French during the baron's revolt in 1217. Orford's importance declined from the time of Edward I (*r.* 1272–1307), who granted it to noblemen. Robert de Ufford, Earl of Suffolk, was given its possession in 1336.

ADDRESS	Orford, Suffolk, East Anglia, England, IP12 2 ND
CONSTRUCTION HISTORY	1163–75
COMMISSIONED BY	Henry II
MATERIALS	Stone, brick and timber
STYLE	Norman donjon

Sir Arthur Churchman presented the castle to the Orford town trust in 1930, from where it eventually passed into guardianship of the British government in 1962. It is now managed and maintained by English Heritage.

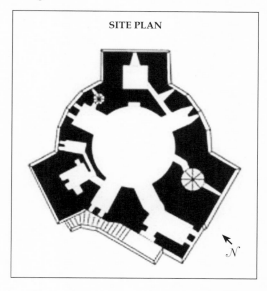

SITE PLAN

Buttressed, multi-angled walls of the donjon negated blind spots or 'dead areas' for the archers at the walls.

The cannon in the castle's foreground..

Facing page:
The high walls of Orford keep stand out in dramatic contrast to the surrounding green countryside.

ENGLAND
Ludlow
London

Ludlow Castle

Flanked by steep slopes on the north and west, and overlooking the river Terne, Ludlow was one of the prominent English defensive castles on the Welsh border during the Middle Ages. Construction was begun in 1085 by the Marcher lord, Roger de Lacy, whose family held the castle for 200 years, after which it passed to the powerful Mortimer family. Ludlow became a crown castle in the 15th century. Under Richard, Duke of York, it was a major center in the War of the Roses. In 1501, Prince Arthur and his new bride, Catherine of Aragon, lived here for briefly until his tragic death in what came to be known as Arthur's Tower. Throughout the 16th and the 17th centuries, Ludlow was also the seat of the Lords President of the Council of Wales—in effect the seat of administration for the March shires and Wales.

The curtain wall of the castle forms a rectangular enclosure, with the main entry from the town on the eastern side. The inner bailey is in the north-west corner, protected by a sloping curtain wall with four square mural towers, and a deep trench. The main residential buildings are in the inner ward, as well as a Norman chapel, with an unusual circular nave.

ADDRESS	Castle Square, Ludlow, Shropshire, England, SY8 1AY
CONSTRUCTION HISTORY	**11th century** Inner bailey with flanking towers and surrounding rock-cut ditch; a T-shaped gatehouse keep with a barrel-vaulted passage
	12th century Gatehouse keep extended to a four-story square donjon; round Norman chapel of St Mary Magdalene within the inner bailey
	13th and 14th century semi-circular Mortimer's Tower; domestic buildings in the inner bailey along the north wall including the Great Hall and Great Chamber, and the square tower in the north wall (later called Arthur's Tower)
	16th century Set of chambers; north gatehouse.
	19th century to date repair and restoration
COMMISSIONED BY	Roger de Lacy
MATERIALS	Silurian limestone
STYLE	Keep and bailey; Norman, Tudor

From the mid-18th century, the castle fell into a state of neglect. The 2nd Earl of Powis purchased it in 1811, and began restoration. At present, it is managed by the trustees of the Powis Castle Estate.

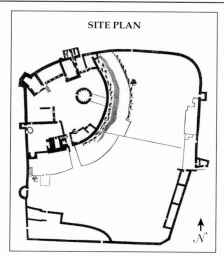

SITE PLAN

N

A drawbridge spans the ditch and leads to the castle gatehouse.

The circular Norman chapel still retains some original decorations.

Facing page:
An aerial view of Ludlow castle: note the sturdy mural towers and wall walk all around the curtain wall.

ENGLAND

London
Dover

Dover Castle

Called the 'Key to England', this formidable castle traces its beginnings to two ancient Roman lighthouses that stood atop the famous white cliffs of Dover. Established by royal charter in 1155, Dover was one of the prominent Cinque Ports. After 1066, William the Conquerer reinforced the remains of a Saxon fortress at this site by new earthworks , and his successor Henry II ordered a giant four-storey Norman keep at an astronomical cost of £6000. Behind its 17–21 ft thick walls were contained the royal chambers, the Great Hall, myriad passages, several tower staircases and a chapel. A 250 ft deep well in the basement supplied water through a network of lead lined pipes.

In 1216, the castellan Hugh de Burgh successfully fended off an attack by the French. By the 13th century, the castle's outer wall extended down to the cliff face. The earlier gatehouse had been replaced by the redoubtable Constable's Gate, which even today is the residence of the Deputy Constable of Dover Castle. The Parliamentarians held the castle briefly in 1642. Underground barracks, constructed during the Napoleonic Wars, were extended during World War II, when the castle served as an air raid shelter, and then a base of military operations during the Dunkirk evacuation. For a brief time, it was also a military hospital.

ADDRESS	Castle Hill, Dover, Kent, England, CT16 HU
CONSTRUCTION HISTORY	**1181–87** Square keep (h. 83 ft); work begun on the outer bailey and curtain wall, three-storey forebuilding
	1199–1216 Outer wall work completed with D-shaped towers; enclosing wall for the Saxon church of St Mary in Castro and Roman lighthouses
	1216 Eastern gateway damaged by mine during French siege.
	1216–72 Castle walls extend down to the cliff face
	1256 Castle at full extent with 20 individual towers
	1800–15 Underground military barracks inside the cliffs; bomb-proof arches in the donjon; outer towers cut down for artillery platforms; Canon's Gateway and Constable's Bastion (west wall)
	Mid-19th century Batteries added; modified later for World War II
COMMISSIONED BY	Henry II (r. 1154-89)
ARCHITECT	**1800s**: Engineer William Twiss (Canon's gateway, Constables Bastion, artillery platforms, underground barracks)
MATERIALS	Sandstone
STYLE	Concentric castle around a square keep

The Lord Warden of the Cinque Ports is officially the Constable of the castle, though it is owned and maintained by English Heritage.

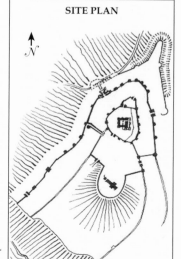

SITE PLAN

Facing page:
Dover has stood sentinel over the coast of England for over a 1000 years.

Peverell's Gateway, one of the main entrances into the castle.

View from the battlements: the Roman Pharos ,the Church of St Mary in Castro, and the sea beyond.

ENGLAND

London

Tower of London

Popularly known as 'The Tower', this is actually a large complex of buildings within a double-walled concentric arrangement, the whole surrounded by a moat. The inner ward has a rectangular high stone keep, St Johns Chapel, numerous towers and residential structures. The phrase 'sent to the Tower' had dreadful implications in English history, as it served as a prison for high-born offenders, many of whom were also executed here. Among these were Anne Boleyn and Thomas More who were brought to the Tower by the infamous 13th century Traitor's Gate. It is also among the most haunted sites in England. Anne's ghost is said to walk in the chapel of St Peter ad Vincula carrying her head under her arm. Other ghosts include those of the two Princes of the Tower, Henry VI, and Lady Jane Grey.

The original keep, built by William the Conqueror in the 11th centurywas whitewashed by his successor Henry II; hence its name 'The White Tower'. In the 13th century Henry III transformed the Tower into a royal residence by adding a new Great hall bounded by the residential Wakefield and Lanthorn towers. Though the Tower ceased to be a royal residence in the 17th century, it continued to house the Royal Mint, record office and Royal menagerie until the 19th century. Till 1855 it was also the royal arsenal. The Crown Jewels of England are on display in the Jewel Tower.

ADDRESS	Tower Hill, EC3N 4 London, UK
CONSTRUCTION HISTORY	**1066–78** First defenses along the old Roman wall; Tower keep and St John's chapel;
	Late 12th century walls expanded;
	1241 Keep whitewashed; stained glass in the chapel;
	1216–72 inner ward enclosed by wall with D-shaped and round mural towers, residential palaces
	1275–85 160 ft wide moat; outer walls with six flanking towers to create a concentric castle; southern wall from reclaimed land; St Thomas's Tower with barbican and moat; Traitors Gate;
	16th century Queens's house;
	19th century Waterloo barracks, Fusiliers Museum;
COMMISSIONED BY	William the Conqueror
ARCHITECTS	Gandulf, Bishop of Rochester (White Tower)
MATERIALS	Kentish ragstone with Caen stone for buttresses and window dressings; wooden floors (White Tower)
STYLE	Keep, concentric castle; Romanesque chapel

The Tower is cared for by an independent charity called Historic Royal Palaces. Yeomen Warders, also known as 'Beefeaters' serve as guards as well as guide visitors through the complex. They are a tourist attraction in themselves and also care for the family of ravens in the tower.

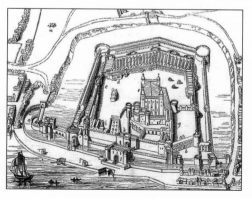

Facing page: the Tower of London has stood at the banks of the Thames River for over nine centuries.

The famous Tower ravens. An ancient legend has it that the kingdom will fall should the ravens ever leave the Tower.

Traitors Gate, through which enemies of the state were escorted into the Tower.

ENGLAND
• Warwick
London

Warwick Castle

Grade I historic building

Warwick castle is situated along a sandstone crest on a bend in the Avon River. The first Norman keep was sacked by Simon de Montford during the baronial rebellion against Henry III in 1264. In the 14th and 15th centuries, a formidable stronghold was built here by the Beauchamps and Nevilles, the influential Earls of Warwick. In 1478, the castle reverted to the crown, and in 1604, James I gave it to the Greville family, who transformed Warwick from a fortress into an elegant country seat.

The old Norman keep on a raised motte on the western side was incorporated into the curtain wall of the new oblong castle bailey in the 14th century. Two impressive towers stand at the north-east and south-east corners. The three-lobed Caesar's Tower has six storeys, with stone vaulting in the interiors. It has two tiers of battlements, the lower level of which are machicolated. The polygonal five-story Guy's Tower has similar vaulted chambers, and a single line of machicolated battlements. The gatehouse of the castle rose to three floors above the gate, and had a crenellated barbican. Living quarters were along the south wall overlooking the river, as this was deemed the most secure location. An underground dungeon existed below.

ADDRESS	Warwick, Warwickshire, England, CV34 4QU
CONSTRUCTION HISTORY	**Pre–11th century** Early Anglo-Saxon fortification.
	1068 Early Norman motte and keep
	12th century Rebuilt as stone octagonal keep
	1264 Castle damaged during Second Baron's War
	1350–1400 Guy's Tower; Caesar's Tower; gatehouse and barbican; domestic quarters
	17th century Interiors refurbished; gardens landscaped
	1871 Damages due to fire
	1872 Restoration of Great Hall and State rooms by Anthony Salvin
COMMISSIONED BY	Earls of Warwick
MATERIALS	Grey sandstone
STYLE	Motte-and-bailey; keep and curtain wall

Once the home of kingmakers and powerful lords, Warwick castle has many legends and resident ghosts. In 1978, it was purchased by the owner's of Madame Tussaud's created a spectacular waxwork tableau to illustrate its history, and opened the castle to the public. Other attractions are the splendid state rooms, ramparts, Armory collection, waxworks and dungeon.

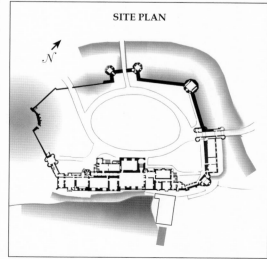

SITE PLAN

Facing page:
Warwick Castle, in the town of Warwick, sits on a sandstone bluff at a bend of the River Avon.

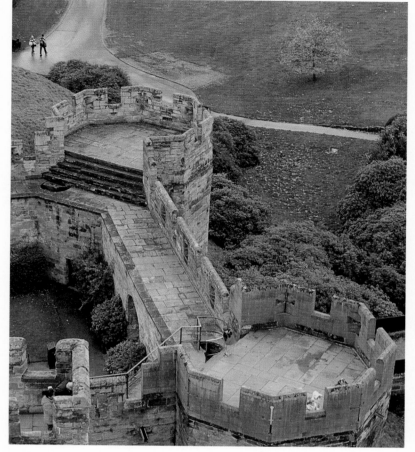

The Bear and Clarence Tower, as seen from Guy's Tower.

The Armory has a vast collection of medieval weapons and armor.

ENGLAND

London

Bodiam

Bodiam Castle

Considered one of the most romantic castles in Britain, Bodiam was built as the private residence of a Sussex knight, Sir Edward Dalyngrigge, in the late 14th century. Sir Edward was a veteran of the wars of Edward III, and was granted permission to fortify his land against the threat of French incursions. Over a span of five years, he created a fairy-tale castle at the center of a gleaming, artificial moat, near the Rother River. The French threat gradually faded away and Bodiam castle saw little or no action until the Civil war, when it was almost destroyed.

The square, symmetrical fortress has a round tower at each corner, a large towered gatehouse in the north wall, and a postern in the south wall. To add to its security, it could only be approached in stages. A bridge from the shore led to an octagonal outwork in the lake. From here a visitor had to cross two drawbridges and a barbican to reach the main gatehouse, all the while being exposed to archers standing at the macholated parapets of the castle. Within the gatehouse, three portcullises led to the inner courtyard. These were made of oak plated with iron, and one of them has survived intact from medieval times. In addition, there were murder holes, called *meurtrière*, in the vaulted ceiling of the gatehouse, through which any unwelcome arrivals could be assaulted with pitch or boiling oil. The gunports on the towers were later additions.

However, once inside the bailey, the enemy had a clear run of the domestic buildings ranged around the inner walls, including a Great Hall, the family solar, bedrooms, kitchens, a chapel and a buttery. In other castles of the time, this was deemed an unsafe arrangement and the main chambers were sited in secure towers.

ADDRESS	Bodiam, Robertsbridge, East Sussex, England, TN32 5UA
CONSTRUCTION HISTORY	**1385–90** Construction of moat and castle
	Civil war Castle dismantled and slighted
	1830–70 Some repairs and survey by owners
	1916 Lord Curzon initiates excavation and restoration work
	1925 National Trust continues restoration
COMMISSIONED BY	Sir Edward Dalyngrigge
MATERIALS	Sandstone
STYLE	Water castle

Bodiam was left to ruin until 1917, when Lord Curzon purchased the castle and took on the task of restoration. He left Bodiam castle to the National Trust in 1925.

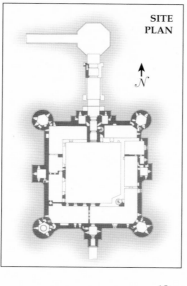

SITE PLAN

N

Facing page:
Bodiam's picturesque setting on an island in an artificial lake.

A medieval portcullis guards the main gateway into the castle.

The southeast corner tower seen through an arrowslit in the curtain wall.

ENGLAND

London

Arundel

Arundel Castle

Bounded by the river Arun on one side and overlooking its namesake town on the other, Arundel is one of the best restored medieval castles in England. The first timber fort and earthworks were built in 1067 by Roger of Montgomery, the first Earl of Arundel. After his death, the title and castle passed to William d'Aubigny. Since then it has been handed down to his descendents, twice through the female line. It occasionally reverted to the Crown, due to the vagaries of political fortune, but came back to the family line. It is now the home of the Fitzalan-Howards, the Roman Catholic Dukes of Norfolk, who are also the hereditary Earl Marshals of England and head of the College of Arms.

The original structure was a stone keep on a high central motte ,with an enclosed bailey on either side. The 14th-century Fitzalan chapel is a masterpiece of English Gothic with an elegant carved timber roof and choir stalls. A glass wall divides the Catholic section from the parish church. The castle suffered heavy damage during the 17th-century Civil War. Repairs were begun in the 18th century and carried on till 1900, when it was modernized with electricity, service lifts, plumbing and heating. Much of the rebuilding followed the lines of the 12th century fortification. The Victorian rooms were commissioned for the Queen's three-day visit in 1846 by the 11th Duke of Norfolk, who also built the magnificent library.

ADDRESS	Arundel Castle, Arundel, West Sussex, BN18 9AB, UK
CONSTRUCTION HISTORY	**1067–1070** Earthwork and timber fort with two wards; stone gatehouse
	1138 Stone shell keep; thick curtain walls with flat buttresses; gate tower in south bailey
	14th century Gate tower heightened and twin-towered barbican added
	1390 Fitzalan chapel
	1642-45 Badly damaged in sieges
	18th century 1900 Repairs begun
	19th century Extensive reconstruction on south side; modern facilities
	Mid-19th century Victorian rooms
	1906 Northeast gateway
COMMISSIONED BY	Earls of Arundel, later Dukes of Norfolk
MATERIALS	Timber and mud; Caen stone; Salisbury limestone
STYLE	Norman motte and double bailey, English Gothic (chapel)

Arundel Castle is managed by a charitable family trust and most of the castle and grounds are open to the public. The castle boasts an enormous collection of art treasures including paintings, fine furniture, arms, tapestries and clocks. At the northeast gateway are the statues of the Howard Lion and the Fitzalan horse brought here in the 1930s from their original location at the Norfolk suspension bridge.

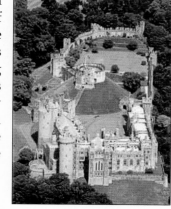

Facing page: Arundel is one of the best restored medieval castles in England.

A carved figure in the interior of the 14th-century Fitzalan chapel.

A birds-eye view of the perimeter wall and the northeast gateway guarded by the Howard lion and the Fitzalan horse.

Bamburgh

ENGLAND

London

Bamburgh Castle

This stunning castle of red sandstone, positioned atop a prominent basalt outcrop on the coast of Northumbria, has been a seat of royal power since early times. It was the coronation site for the kings of Northumbria. Evidence shows occupation in the Roman era, and it was very likely an ancient Briton stronghold. The first fort at this vantage site was built in 550 CE by the Anglo-Saxon chieftain Ida the Flamebearer. His grandson Ethelfrith gave the castle to his wife Bebba, from whom it derived the name Bebbanburgh, which later simplified to Bamburgh. In 935 CE, it was attacked and left in ruins by the Vikings. The present stone keep was built by the Normans in the 11th century, and for the next four centuries, Bamburgh remained an impregnable bastion of English strength along the precarious Scottish border.

In the War of the Roses, Bamburgh was held by the Lancastrians, and besieged by the Yorkists supporter, Richard Neville, the Earl of Warwick. The castle was forced to yield to heavy cannon fire and suffered considerable damage. By the 17th century, most of the medieval structure was in ruins, save the sturdy keep. It was purchased in 1894 by Lord Armstrong, a Victorian industrialist and enthusiastic scientist who undertook a massive restoration program. He also built the spectacular Kings Hall on the site of the earlier Great Hall. Today the castle displays a fascinating collection of medieval armory and artifacts, along with the noteworthy Armstrong and Aviation Museum.

A view of the clock tower, formerly called the Belle Tower. Note the mix of the earlier red stone with grey stone, which was used in repairs conducted by Lord Armstrong.

ADDRESS	Bamburgh, Northumberland, NE69 7DF
CONSTRUCTION HISTORY	**Sixth century** Anglo-Saxon fort
	11th century Walled keep
	1464 Walls and outbuildings heavily damaged by cannon fire during siege
	By 17th century Only keep survives intact
	18th century Keep restored and modified
	20th century Extensive reconstruction; Kings Hall
COMMISSIONED BY	Henry II
MATERIALS	Red sandstone
STYLE	Keep and bailey; Norman

The castle is still owned by the Armstrong family. The Bamburgh Castle Research project was begun in 1996 to promote an understanding of the archaeology and history of Bamburgh and its environment. It conducts summer workshops for students and archaeology enthusiasts.

Facing page:
Situated on the dramatic coast of Northumbria at the edge of English border, Bamburgh Castle has witnessed innumerable battles since ancient times.

The 18th century windmill located at the far end of the castle keep.

ENGLAND

London

Carisbrooke

Carisbrooke Castle

Tracing its roots to an ancient Roman fort, Carisbrooke has been witness to 1200 years of turbulent history. A Norman motte and bailey was built in the 11th century. This was gradually expanded into a polygonal keep, curtain wall and gatehouse by the Redvers family that controlled the castle until 1293, when it was sold to King Edward I. Successive Crown-appointed wardens added to the keep, domestic buildings and the fortifications. It was unsuccessfully attacked by the French in 1377. The threat of the Spanish Armada in the 16th century induced the Governor Sir George Carey to commission elaborate artillery earthworks by the Italian military engineer Federigo Gianibelli. It was restored and re-consecrated in 1904. Charles I was imprisoned in the castle for 14 months before his execution in 1649, and his room in the Constable's chamber is also a popular attraction.

Two wells served the castle, one of which is still operated in the bailey by a donkey-drawn wheel, much to the delight of young visitors. The other well is up in the keep, accessed by a steep flight of 71 steps. The beautiful 13th century chapel of St Nicholas in Castro was built by Countess Isabella de Fortibus, the last member of the Redvers family to live in the castle.

ADDRESS	Castle Hill, Newport, Isle of Wight, PO30 1, UK
CONSTRUCTION HISTORY	**11th century** Motte and bailey
	12th century Polygonal keep on artificial mound; stone curtain walls; square flanking towers in southeast and southwest
	13th century Domestic buildings including the Great Hall; chapel
	14th century Twin-towered gatehouse
	15th century Woodville gate
	16th century Massive artillery earthworks
	1904 Chapel restored
COMMISSIONED BY	The Redvers family
MATERIALS	Earth, rubble, timber and stone
STYLE	Keep and bailey; Norman, Elizabethan defenses

The Carisbrooke Castle Museum was opened in 1898 by the Island Governor Princess Beatrice, youngest daughter of Queen Victoria, in memory of her late husband, Prince Henry of Battenburg. Initially centered on exhibits related to Charles I, it has expanded since to focus on the entire history of human settlement on the island.

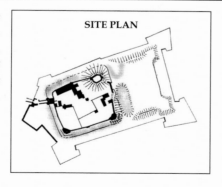

SITE PLAN

English Heritage maintains Carisbrooke Castle and also provides a holiday flat within the castle since 2007.

Facing page:
Carisbrooke has been the site of a stronghold since the 8th century, and faced the threat of numerous invaders from the 10th century Vikings to the 16th century Spanish.

The elegant 13th century chapel, St Nicholas in Castro, after its restoration in 1904.

The window in the castle tower through which Charles I attempted to escape.

ENGLAND

London

Leeds

Leeds Castle

Set in tranquil surroundings on three connected islands amid a gleaming lake in Kent, Leeds castle was once the Saxon manor of Esledes. It was fortified in stone by the Norman knight Robert de Crevecouer, and by the end of the 13th century, Edward I had transformed it into a royal palace for his wife, Eleanor of Castile. Leeds castle and its surrounding acres became part of the Queen's Dower, and were held by five other queens of England, namely, Margaret of France, Isabella of France, Joan of Navarre, Anne of Bohemia and Catharine de Valois. It was one of the favored royal residences, especially in Tudor times. Henry VIII entertained here lavishly with his vast entourage, and even retreated to its peaceful surroundings to escape the plague in London in 1528.

The architecture spans 800 years. Edward I built the bounding wall with D-shaped towers and the exceptionally strong barbican. His inner keep, also known as the Gloriette, was refurbished in grand style by Henry VIII. In 1552, Edward VI gave the castle as a reward to Sir Anthony de Leger, for his services in Ireland. Leeds survived destruction in the Civil War as its owners, the Culpepper family, fortunately supported the Parliamentarians. They were also the creators of the famous Culpepper Gardens. The last owner, Lady Baillie, employed the French architect Armand-Albert Rateau to oversee extensive alterations and install sumptuous interiors.

ADDRESS	Leeds Castle, Maidstone, Kent ME17 1PL
CONSTRUCTION HISTORY	**10th century** Saxon manor house
	1199 Stone fortifications
	13th century External riveting wall with towers; stone keep; fortified millhouse; barbican in three sections, each with its gateway, drawbridge and portcullis
	16th century Renovations to the bailey buildings and keep
	17th century The Culpepper garden
	20th century Extensive repair and redecoration
COMMISSIONED BY	Edward I
ARCHITECT	Armand-Albert Rateau (20th century modifications)
MATERIALS	Stone
STYLE	Norman, Tudor, Jacobean (interiors)

The castle was opened to the public in 1976. Extensive grounds cover 500 acres and include an aviary, a maze, a grotto and a golf course. The Leeds Castle foundation manages the castle, and organizes many events and festivals through the year.

Facing page:
Its peaceful setting and safe location made Leeds a favorite royal castle, the site of feasts and hunting-parties.

A view of the two-story Gloriette, or the Lady's Castle, built by Edward I for his queen, Eleanor of Castile. It is connected to the rest of the castle by an arched bridge.

The tastefully appointed interiors of the castle library are a result of 20th century restoration.

ENGLAND

London

Tintagel

Tintagel Castle

Located on a windswept isthmus of black slate on the coast of Cornwall, Tintagel is indelibly associated with the romantic tales of King Arthur and the Knights of the Round Table. The legend originated in Geoffrey of Monmouth's 13th century treatise, *History of the Kings of Great Britain*, which wove the myth of Arthur's extraordinary life, and ascribed his birthplace to be the mysterious Celtic bastion of Tintagel. Inspired by this account, and also hopeful of local acceptance of his overlordship, Lord Richard of Cornwall built a castle on this isolated spot in 1240. Having little strategic value, it was ignored by his descendents, and fell rapidly to ruin. Very little remains today of the original walls and pillars. In Victorian days, it became a popular tourist destination, and was maintained by local initiative, which provided a guide service for visitors.

Historians now believe that Arthur was a Romano-British warrior leading the resistance to the Saxon invaders of the sixth century. Archaeological evidence has revealed a hoard of fine Mediterranean pottery, which is indicative of luxurious occupation and trade from the fifth century. This gives credence to the popular belief that Tintagel is the seat of the ancient kings of Cornwall.

The ruins are reached by two steep staircases along the hillside. A clifftop path leads to Tintagel church, which dates to early Norman times. Nearby is Merlin's Cave, and a footpath called 'Arthurs Way' that takes the adventurous visitor to Cadbury Castle, another Arthurian stronghold in Cornwall.

ADDRESS	Tintagel Castle, Tintagel, Cornwall, PL 34 0HE, England
CONSTRUCTION PERIOD	*c.* 1240
COMMISSIONED BY	Richard, Duke of Cornwall
MATERIALS	Devon slate
STYLE	Rock castle

Lord Alfred Tennyson carried on the Arthurian legend in *Idylls of the King* (1856–85). *Tintagel Castle* was the name of one of the ships in the Union-Castle shipping line, and also a locomotive of the Great Western Railway. At present it is in the care of English Heritage.

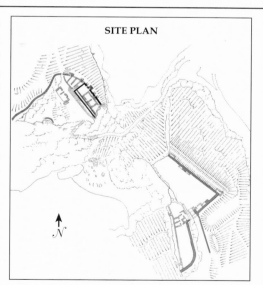

SITE PLAN

N

A doorway in the castle looks out on to a spectacular view of the Cornish countryside.

Crumbling walls are all that have survived of the medieval castle.

Facing page:
A steep staircase winds its way up to the ruined castle, perched at the very edge of the escarpment. Steeped in myth and magic, Tintagel is evocative of a bygone age of heroes, honor and chivalry.

ENGLAND

London

Windsor

Windsor Castle

Windsor holds a special place in the hearts of the English monarchy, so much so that George V chose Windsor as the family surname in 1917. The first wooden castle was built by William the Conqueror on the plan of a central motte with a bailey on either side. Henry II rebuilt it in stone, and the internal buildings were added by Edward III in the 14th century. Being a day's ride from London, Windsor was always a favored royal residence, and successive monarchs added to and altered the interiors to their taste. Ten monarchs are buried in the magnificent Chapel of St George, built in the late 15th century. The apartments were lavishly decorated by Charles II, who also laid out the Long Walk. A massive rebuilding and renovation programme took place in the 1820's under the architect Jeffry Wyatville, who designed the formal East Terrace gardens. A chapel dating to 1485 was converted into the Albert Memorial Chapel by Queen Victoria in 1863.

The castle is one of the most visited places in England. Among its highlights are the State Apartments with their splendid furnishings, the Royal Collection which includes works by Michelangelo and Holbein, the dignified St George's Hall, and the impressive Waterloo chamber which is lined with portraits of England's heroes. Also on display is Queen Mary's Dolls' House designed by Edwin Lutyens in 1924.

The lovely Gothic façade of St. Georges Chapel, birthplace of the Order of the Garter. The annual ceremony of the Order still takes place here.

ADDRESS	Castle Hill, Windsor, Windsor and Maidenhead SL4 1, UK
CONSTRUCTION HISTORY	*c.* **1070** Wooden motte and bailey
	1154–89 Shell keep in stone called the Round Tower
	1327–77 Domestic buildings in the baileys including St Georges Hall
	1475–1528 Chapel of St George
	1660–85 Long Walk; State Apartments redone; St George's Hall with ceilings by Antonio Verro and carvings by Gibbons
	1820–30 Keep heightened, buttressed and battlemented; State Apartments renovated; East Terrace gardens;
	1863 Albert Memorial Chapel;
COMMISSIONED BY	rulers of England
ARCHITECTS	William of Wykeham (14th century); Hugh May (17th century); Jeffry Wyatville (19th century)
MATERIALS	Timber, stone
STYLE	Norman keep and bailey; St Georges Chapel: Perpendicular Gothic; interiors: Tudor, Stuart, Georgian and Victorian

Windsor is one of the official residences of the Queen, and the royal family often spends the weekend here. Frogmore Estate which lies within the Home Park of the Castle, is the burial place of Prince Albert and Queen Victoria.

Facing page:
A royal residence and one of England's most well-known sights, Windsor has been fully restored after a disastrous fire swept through the State Apartments in 1992.

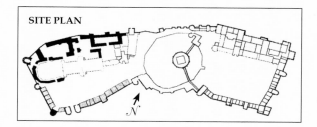

SITE PLAN

The Round Tower dating to 11th century now houses the Royal Archives and Photographic Collection.

ENGLAND

JERSEY ISLAND — Mont Orgueil

Mont Orgueil Castle

Mont Orgueil was constructed in the 12th century to defend Jersey Island from the French after the division of the Duchy of Normandy in 1204. The castle was the main seat of administration of the English governors of Jersey. Located on a hill overlooking the Gorey harbor, it is also known as Gorey Castle or *Le Vièr Châté* by the inhabitants of this picturesque island. It was a key defense against the French for centuries, until the invention of gunpowder rendered it vulnerable to attack from adjacent high spots such as Mount Saint Nicholas. In the 16th century, its defensive role was further reduced by the construction of a new fortification, called Elizabeth castle off St Helier. However, Mont Orgueil remained the island prison until the end of the 17th century.

By 1700, the castle was in a dilapidated state, and abandoned as a prison. It was subsequently refitted as a garrison, and in 1800 Admiral Phillipe d'Auvergne used the Corbelled Tower as a headquarters for his undercover operations in Brittany and Normandy. The castle remembers several royal visits with pride; Queen Victoria visited the castle in 1846, as did George V and Elizabeth II. Traditionally, up until the 19th century, Mont Orgueil was opened to the public on Easter Monday, when crowds flocked to the St Georges chapel within its walls. The castle was handed over to the People of Jersey on June 28, 1907. It has been managed as a museum since 1929, barring the years of German occupation in World War II.

The gun platforms built by the occupying German army during World War II.

ADDRESS	Gorey, St Martin, JE3 6ET
CONSTRUCTION HISTORY	13th century
	1204 Construction of castle
	17th century repairs and construction of garrison quarters
	1800 Corbelled Tower renovated for use
	1929 converted to museum
	World War II modern fortifications by the Germans
	2006 extensive building and restoration completed; weatherproof elements added; new visitor attractions
COMMISSIONED BY	rulers of England
MATERIALS	xxxxxxx
STYLE	Rock castle

Since 1994, the castle has been managed by the Jersey Heritage Trust. In 2006 the castle reopened after an extensive rebuilding and restoration plan. A newly designed exhibition displays the 800-year history of the castle. Many parts of the castle have been reconstructed and weatherproofed. A Living History section is also part of the exhibition from April to October each year.

Facing page:
The imposing bulk of Mont Orgueil overlooks the fishing boats and pier at Gorey harbor. It was virtually impregnable till the advent of artillery.

The bell tower on the castle ramparts.

Gisors
•
Paris

FRANCE

Château de Gisors

Château de Gisors is situated in the heart of the Vexin region in northern France, an area that was long disputed between the Norman dukes and the kings of France. Its origin dates to the 11th century, when the motte with a shell keep and tower was built by William Rufus, and his sons Henry I and II, who were the Kings of England as well as Dukes of Normandy. However, Richard the Lionheart lost the castle to Philip Augustus, the Capetian king of France in 1193. The last Grand Master of the Templars, Jacques de Molay, was imprisoned for a time at Gisors in the early 14th century. The castle changed hands several times in the Hundred Years War, before finally falling into French hands towards the end of the conflict.

The polygonal shell keep atop a high earthen motte is reached by a steep flight of stairs. The walls of the keep were originally bonded with timber ties in the masonry and its angles strengthened by small pilaster buttresses. It contained within an octagonal donjon and a small Romanesque chapel (dedicated to Thomas Becket) as well as a kitchen area. The circular three-story Prisoner's Tower was added by the French after 1193. The motte itself was enclosed by a loosely rectangular outer bailey wall protected by a moat and earthworks. A barbican opened into the adjacent fortified town. In the 14th century, casemates were built along the wall to protect the base of the wall. The bailey was spacious enough to easily accommodate a large garrison that could either defend the town, or in the case of a popular uprising, protect those inside the castle from the townspeople.

Gisors' multi-angled shell wall encloses an octagonal tower.

ADDRESS	Château de Gisors, Rue de Penthièvre 27140 Gisors
CONSTRUCTION HISTORY	**1096** Motte built by William Rufus
	12th century Elliptical shell wall with pilaster buttresses, octagonal tower, chapel (1184), outer bailey and barbican
	1206 Prisoner's Tower
	14th century Casemates
COMMISSIONED BY	Kings of England
MATERIALS	Stone and timber
STYLE	Shell keep in motte and bailey (donjon included later)

The Château de Gisors is an excellent example of early medieval military architecture. It is open to the public.

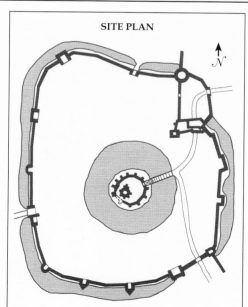

SITE PLAN

Facing page:
One of the most perfect examples of a shell keep, Gisors was one of the oft disputed castles between the Dukes of Normandy and the French kings.

The circular castle yard.

Falaise • Paris •

FRANCE

Château de Falaise

The ancestral seat of the Dukes of Normandy, Falaise castle lies on the Ante river, 12.5 miles (20 km) south-west of Caen. It is famous as the birthplace of William the Conqueror, the first Norman king of England. According to legend, Duke Robert the Magnificent was besotted by Arlette, the tanner's daughter, whom he met near the stream below the castle while returning from a hunt. Their son Guillame (or William) was born in the autumn of 1027. Despite being recognized as the legal heir, he was nicknamed William the Bastard. After his successful conquest of England, the Norman lords in France continued to retain their fiefs and titles in Normandy. Falaise remained in the control of William's successors until they were decisively evicted by Phillip II of France in 1204.

The high-walled rectangular keep at Falaise was built around 1120 by Henry I of England, the youngest son of Duke William. The massive cylindrical donjon next to it was erected by Philip II after 1204. During the Hundred Years Wars Falaise changed hands several times, and cannon-ports were added on its battlements by the English. The round tower was damaged in battle and repaired by the English commander, after whom it is called Talbot's Tower. Toward the end of the 16th century, the western walls were damaged by cannon fire, and by the 18th century the castle was abandoned. There was heavy fighting around the Falaise Gap in World War II, but the castle escaped serious damage.

ADDRESS	Château de Falaise, 14700 Falaise, Basse-Normandie, France
CONSTRUCTION HISTORY	**10th century** First stone keep
	1120s Rectangular donjon; corner chapel
	13th century Round tower
	1337–1453 Castle damaged and repaired
COMMISSIONED BY	Henry I of England
MATERIALS	Stone
STYLE	Romanesque keep; round donjon

Restoration work has been underway since the 1980s, and the castle was opened to the public in 1997.

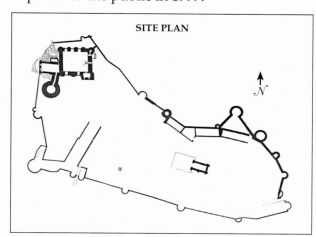

SITE PLAN

N

Facing page:
Built on a rock escarpment, Falaise is one of the most significant tower keeps of the 12th century. It was the birthplace of William of Normandy, also known as William the Conqueror for his conquest of England in 1066.

Philip II's massive round donjon looms over the square keep built by Henry I of England.

The castle as seen from the town.

Loches

Paris

Loches
FRANCE

Château de Loches

The Château de Loches is located at the summit of a rocky hill next to the river Indre in the verdant Loire valley of central France. It was part of the domain of the Counts of Anjou and finds a mention in the sixth century *Historia Francorum* (History of the Franks) of Gregory of Tours. The earliest stone structure was probably built in the reign of the fearsome Count Fulk Nerra, who extensively fortified his lands in his brutal wars against the Counts of Blois. It was part of the Angevin holdings of the English kings, which were reclaimed by Philip II in 1204, whereupon Loches became a French royal castle. It was the favored residence of Charles VII who built the *Logis Royal* (Royal Lodge) for his mistress, Agnès Sorel. It was here that he received the triumphant Joan of Arc after her victory against the English in 1429. His son, Louis XI, converted Loches into a state prison, and its dungeons contain iron cages believed to have been used to house important prisoners. The castle was ransacked and but only slightly damaged during the French Revolution.

The massive rectangular keep was commissioned by Henry II of England; his successor Richard rebuilt it with 9 ft (3 m) thick walls rising to a lofty 122 ft (37 m). The walls were provided with semi-circular buttresses, and a forebuilding guarded the entrance. As in all stone keeps, the windows are narrow and small, as safety was more important than light. Philip II of France added towers *en bec* to the wall. The Royal Lodge has some fine tapestries and furnishings.

ADDRESS	Château de Loches 27600 Loches
CONSTRUCTION HISTORY	**Ninth century** Stone keep
	10th–12th century Collegiate Church of St Ours (finished in 15th century)
	11th–12th century Four-story rectangular keep with a basement cross wall; cylindrical buttresses, three-story forebuilding with chapel
	13th century *En bec* towers; Royal Gate begun
	15th century Royal Lodge; tomb of Agnes Sorrel
COMMISSIONED BY	Henry II of England
MATERIALS	Stone
STYLE	donjon, bailey castle

The Château of Loches is one of the better preserved of medieval castles in France. The Collegiate Church of St Ours is well-known for its fantastical carvings over the doorway, two unusual pyramidal towers and the tomb of Agnès Sorel.

SITE PLAN

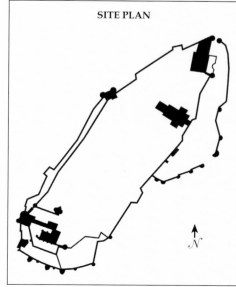

Facing page:
The passage leading to the main entrance of the château. The main keep towers behind it.

The Logis Royal or the Royal Lodge.

A glass painting of Agnès Sorel who is buried at Loches.

Paris
Provins
FRANCE

Château de Provins

The Château de Provins in the Ile-de-France is located at the junction of the rivers Voulzie and Dureint. Its famous donjon, called Tour de Cesar, was built by Theobalt, Count of Champagne, in the 12th century. In 1285, Provins was seized by Philip the Bold of France during his conquest of Champagne. It remained in royal hands until captured by the English in the Hundred Years War in the mid-14th century. The surrounding circular wall, called Pâté aux Anglais, was built by one of the English captains, Thomas Guerand, who dismantled nearby houses for building material.

Placed upon an earthen mound, the donjon has a very distinct and unusual design, as it rises from a rectangular base but converts midway into an octagonal structure. Four semi-circular turrets are snugly fitted at the corners. It has two floors, and a drawbridge connects the top floor of the keep to the wall walk in the *chemise* wall. While the inside of the upper floor has a vaulted dome ceiling, the exterior is flat roofed. This floor contains the Great Hall and the turret chambers. In an interesting departure from the norm, a circular opening in the ceiling allows light into the central chamber. The lower floor or the basement leads further down to the castle well. Mural passages connected the different floors and chambers. It is unclear when the conical roofs were made, but it likely that they date to the 17th century. All but one of the tower bells were melted for arms and money in the years following the French Revolution of 1789.

ADDRESS	Chemin de Villecran, 77482 Provins, France
CONSTRUCTION HISTORY	**12th century** Stone keep
	15th century Surrounding circular wall
	17th century Conical roofs
MATERIALS	Stone
STYLE	Donjon castle

In the middle ages, Provins was one of the six towns where the famous Champagne fairs were held. At present, the castle is open to the public and at the center of a planned effort to preserve and showcase the medieval heritage of the town.

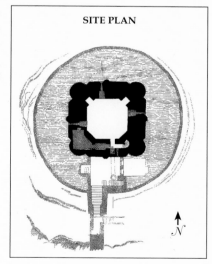

SITE PLAN

The unusually shaped donjon named the Tour de Cesar.

The large bell in the donjon belfry.

Facing page:
The walls of Château de Provins are called Pâté aux Anglais.

Château Gaillard

Richard the Lionheart built a spectacular castle high above a bend in the river Seine in Normandy. Inspired by the crusader forts of the Holy Land, it heralded a major step forward in medieval military architecture, from fortified donjons to concentric castles. Virtually impregnable, it was conquered by the French after a bitter siege in 1203. It gradually fell into disuse and was dismantled by Henry IV at the end of the 16th century. Archeological excavations were conducted at Château-Gaillard in the 1990s.

Château-Gaillard consists of three walled baileys surrounded by dry ditches. The donjon is located at the highest point in the innermost bailey, backed by a steep cliff. It is *en bec*, with one side thickened and drawn out to a sharp angle, which was a strong deterrent to enemy sappers and battering rams. Another unusual feature is the corrugation on the exterior wall face of the inner bailey. This effectively eliminated any blind spots for the archers shooting from the ramparts. Château-Gaillard was also the first in Western Europe to use machicolations in the battlements, an element that became commonplace in later castles.

Roger de Lacy held the castle for King John when the French besieged it and the accompanying town of Les Andelys in 1203. They dug trenches around the lower bailey and prepared to starve out the castle inhabitants, who included soldiers as well as many townspeople. As food ran short, several hundred women, children and the infirm were let out from the gate, but the French refused to let them pass. These unfortunate souls perished of cold and hunger in the dry ditch around the walls. Eventually, the French overtook the castle by undermining the outer bailey wall, and then finding a way into the middle bailey through the castle latrines. The garrison retreated to the donjon and surrendered after a hard -fought battle.

ADDRESS	BP 506 27700, Les Andelys, Haute-Normandie, France
CONSTRUCTION HISTORY	**1196** Construction of the castle (The two towns of Les Andelys were also built at the same time) **1203–04** Outer wall undermined in siege by French; buildings fired **1599** Castle dismantled on orders of Henry IV of France.
COMMISSIONED BY	Richard I, King of England and Duke of Normandy (1189–99)
MATERIALS	Grey sandstone
STYLE	Proto-concentric castle, keep

The château is in ruins today, with just scattered remnants of its once valiant fortifications standing watch over the town below. It is open to the public.

SITE PLAN

↓
N

Facing page:
Richard the Lionheart's stronghold situated atop a high escarpment was a landmark in medieval castle construction.

The imposing bulk of the inner keep, now in ruins.

Corrugating the wall was a novel way to eliminate blind spots during enemy attack.

Paris
FRANCE
Carcassonne

Cité de Carcassonne

The medieval fortified town of Carcassonne stands on the foundations of an ancient Roman settlement, later occupied by Visigoths. A stone curtain wall and castle was erected here in the 11th century, and was considerably expanded over the next 200 years by the Trencavel family, who were the reigning Counts of Carcassonne. Raymond-Roger de Trencavel sheltered the Cathars during the Albegensian Crusades in the early 13th century. In 1209, a crusading army, led by the legendary Simon de Montford, besieged the city and forced its surrender. In 1247, the town was handed back to the French crown and it became an invincible royal bastion guarding the border with Aragon. During the Hundred Years War, Edward the Black Prince made and unsuccessful attempt to take the keep, and instead set fire to the bourg.

Under Trencavel rule the city reached its full medieval splendor. It consisted of a double ring of ramparts covering 1.8 miles (three km), 53 towers, a turreted gateway, a cathedral and a protected inner keep. By the late 17th century, the castle had lost its military importance and was on the verge of being demolished. It obtained a new lease of life in 1853 when Eugène Viollet-le-Duc, the pioneer of architectural conservation, took up its cause and initiated restoration work.

ADDRESS	11000, Carcassonne, France
CONSTRUCTION HISTORY	**First century BCE** Roman fortified town of Carcassonne
	Fifth century CE Visigoths extended the fortress
	12th century Walls, towers, and gateways, the Château Comtal, the Basilica of St Nazaire
	1247–87 Extensive additions and repairs
	1853 Extra buildings against the walls demolished, buildings retiled and decorations recovered, Basilica of St Nazaire and St Celse restored
	1960s Gallo-Roman towers topped with tiles
COMMISSIONED BY	Counts of Carcassonne (11–13th century)
MATERIALS	Stone
STYLE	Fortified town

The cobblestone streets and well-preserved buildings of Carcassonne afford a glimpse of life in the Middle Ages. Of particular interest are the Basilica of St Nazaire and St Celse (now restored to its Gothic elegance), the 14th century Cathedral of St Michel and the Narbonne Gate.

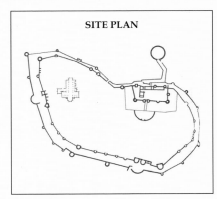

SITE PLAN

Facing page:
The gloriusly illuminated medieval ramparts of Carcassone, considered impregnable in their time.

The picturesque houses with red roofs and the turreted wall date back to 13th century.

The cobblestone passage leading to the main entrance of the fortified town.

Paris
Saumur
FRANCE

Château de Saumur

Surrounded by the verdant vineyards of the Loire valley, the Château Saumur is a strong and graceful edifice located at the confluence of the Loire and the Thouet rivers. There is not much trace of the original 10th century castle from the time of Count Fulk Nerra of Anjou. A royal castle from the 12th century, Saumur changed hands several times in the fluctuating political climate of the Middle Ages. It was lavishly rebuilt by the Duc de Berry in the 14th century. In 1589, it was occupied by the Huguenot thinker Philippe Duplessis-Mornay. From the 1620s it was used as an army barracks, and Napoleon converted it to a prison. The château was acquired by the city of Saumur in 1906, which began its restoration and also established a museum of decorative arts and armor.

Like other buildings in the region, the castle is built of the soft grey local stone called taffeau. The 15th century *Trés Riches Heures* of the Duc de Berry has an illustation of Saumur on the page for September. It is shown as a tall structure with octagonal towers and crenellated battlements, embellished with stained glass windows, Gothic tracery, flying turrets and golden weathercocks. There are still traces of its original fairytale appearance, though the fleurs-de-lys atop the merlons have long since vanished.

ADDRESS	Château de Saumur BP 300 49400 Saumur
CONSTRUCTION HISTORY	**10th century** The first castle
	11th–13th century Destroyed and rebuilt
	14th century Renovations and elaborate decoration in the Renaissance style
COMMISSIONED BY	Count Fulk Nerra
MATERIALS	Taffeau
STYLE	Gothic and remaissance

The town of Saumur has a long standing equestrian history, and the castle also houses the Museum of the Horse. Other attractions include the dungeon, and a collection of antique toys and figurines. It also has a fine collection of 16th-18th century French ceramics.

The folio for September from the 15th century Trés Riches Heures of the Duc de Berry shows what the castle looked like at its height.

Facing page:
Saumur is one of the oldest and most striking castles in the verdant Loire valley, which is famous for its historic châteaux.

A view of the castle from across the river Loire.

Paris

Angers

FRANCE

Château d'Angers

The redoubtable Château d'Angers is the largest of the royal castles in the Loire valley. It is located within the town of Angers, on a slight rise overlooking the river Maine. The estate was part of the Angevin empire of the Plantagenet kings of England, but was wrested back by Philip II of France in 1204. The château was built during the minority of his grandson Louis (later Louis IX) by his mother and Regent, Blanche of Castile. In 1352, the enormous castle was granted to Louis, Duke of Anjou, who commissioned the extraordinary *Apocalypse Tapestry* from the painter Hennequin de Bruges, and the tapestry weaver Nicolas Bataille. His son, Louis II, built the Chapelle St Genevieve, which is said to hold a relic of the True Cross. Henry III of France had the towers reduced, and reportedly used the stone to pave the streets of Angers. Artillery was introduced into the defenses, and the château survived a major siege and bombardment in the wars in the Vendées in the 1790s. A military academy was established at Angers, where ironically, Arthur Wellesley, Duke of Wellington, received his military training, which no doubt served him well in his campaigns against Napoleon.

Unlike the other graceful castles of the Loire, Angers presents a formidable picture of martial strength. The castle's curtain wall had 17 enormous drum towers, with wide plinths to deter sapping. It had two towered gatehouses, and the wall was also connected to the town's fortifications. A deep moat encircled the castle. The only tower that was not reduced by Henry III is the Tour de Moulins, which gives us an idea of the original appearance of the castle. Most of the royal apartments and gardens date to the 16th century.

The elegant chapel and a gateway in the castle keep.

ADDRESS	49100 Angers, France
CONSTRUCTION HISTORY	**1230s** original castle and walls
	14th century Saint-Chapelle
	16th century Palaces, Chatelet; ornamental gardens
	17th century fortifications modified
	1939–45 severely damaged
COMMISSIONED BY	Blanche of Castile, Regent to Louis IX of France
ARCHITECTS	Louis de Vau (domestic ranges, 17th century)
MATERIALS	Schist and limestone
STYLE	Château; French Gothic, Renaissance

Owned by city of Angers, the castle is open to the public, and houses a museum with the largest collection of medieval tapestries in the world, including the invaluable *Apocalypse Tapestry*, depicting the revelation of St John. Large sections of the château were damaged in a fire in 2009, and subsequently rebuilt.

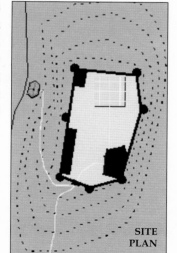

SITE PLAN

Facing page:
The enormous drum towers of the Château d'Angers are less in size today than they were in the 13th century, but they still give an impression of strength and military might.

The remarkable Apocalypse Tapestry on display at the castle museum.

Paris

Vincennes

FRANCE

Château de Vincennes

The enormous royal castle of Vincennes in the Ile de Paris was originally a 12th century hunting lodge, but it grew to become the principal residence of the French monarchs. By the 14th century, the colossal donjon was furnished with regal chambers, and its barbican housed the extensive library of Charles V, who also began construction of the Saint-Chapelle. Vincennes was the birthplace of many monarchs and several were married here. During the Hundred Years War, Henry V of England died here after contracting dysentery following the siege of Meaux in 1422. The 15th century *Trés Riches Heures* of the Duc de Berry features the Château de Vincennes on the folio for the month of December, when hunting parties are held.

When the court moved to Versailles, the castle served as a porcelain factory and a state prison. Nicholas Fouquet, Diderot, Mirabeau and Bonnie Prince Charles were imprisoned here. In 1791, a large mob attacked Vincennes in response to rumors that it was being refitted to incarcerate the revolutionaries.

At its height, Vincennes rivaled the Pope's fortress at Avignon in size and grandeur. The outer courtyard measuring 1096ft by 604ft (334m into 56m) could house a small army. The entire outer wall was battlemented, and the tall donjon had two levels of machicolations and six floors of vaulted chambers lined with wood paneling. A wet moat surrounded the entire outer perimeter. The elegant stained glass windows at Saint-Chapelle were created in 1555 by the master glassmaker Nicholas Beaurain. Two domestic ranges were built by Louis de Vau in the 17th century. Viollet-le-Duc was retained to restore the keep and chapel in the 19th century.

ADDRESS	1 Avenue de Paris, 94300 Vincennes
CONSTRUCTION HISTORY	**12th century** Hunting lodge
	13th century First keep and courtyard
	1337–67 Giant donjon 216ft (66m) high with four corner towers
	1370–80 Donjon enclosed with a barbican, corner turrets and moat; second, much larger enceinte enclosed by a new curtain wall with rectangular towers. The first keep and enclosure lie on its western side.
	17th century Domestic ranges
	19th century Park landscaped; keep and chapel restored
COMMISSIONED BY	Kings of France
MATERIALS	Limestone, timber (roofing, paneling)
STYLE	Moated bailey with keep

The château was the headquarters of the Chief of Staff of the Armed Forces between 1936-40. Germans occupied it between 1940-44. It is now in the charge of the Defense Historical Service of France, which maintains a museum in the keep.

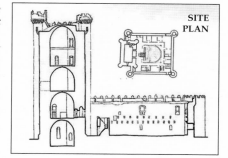

SITE PLAN

Facing page:
The royal castle of Vincennes was the preferred residence of the monarchs until eclipsed in favor by the Palace at Versailles in the 18th century.

The tall barbican was a fortification by itself, set within the walls of a larger enclosure that could accommodate thousands of soldiers.

Detail of the tracery on the exquisite façade of Saint-Chapelle.

FRANCE

Paris

Avignon

Palais de Papes

In 1309, a disputed election and constant factional strife compelled Pope Clement V to shift the Papal Curia from Rome to Avignon, thus inaugurating the period of the Avignon papacy that lasted till 1377. In 1334, Pope Benedict began construction of a new Papal Palace on a rocky outcrop overlooking the river Rhone. It speaks volumes for the uncertain times that the immense Gothic structure, comprising the austere Palais Vieux and the more opulent Palais Neuf, resembles a gigantic fortress rather than a place of peaceful worship. Sumptuous furnishings, frescoes, tapestries and wood paneling reflected the wealth and luxurious lifestyle of the papacy. Several anti-popes continued to reign in Avignon even after Urban V returned the papacy to Rome in 1377. The Palais was sacked by revolutionaries in 1791, and subsequently converted to a barracks and prison during Napoleon's First Empire. Its deterioration continued unabated until 1906, when it was turned into a museum.

The entire complex covers 2.6 acres (11,000 sq m) and was heavily defended by ten towers and machicolated battlements. The Palais Vieux comprises the first phase of construction, and includes the bell tower, the Trouillas Tower, and Benedict XII's cloister with the Benedictine chapel. The adjoining Palais Neuf consists of the Great Chapel, the Great Audience Hall, and several towers around a large courtyard called the Court d'Honneur. Clement VI's study, known as the Stag Room, has beautiful 14th century frescoes and intricate ceramic tiles.

A view of the historic papal complex from across the river Rhone.

ADDRESS	Rue Gérard Philipe 84000 Avignon, France
CONSTRUCTION HISTORY	**1334–42** Palais Vieux
	1342–52 Palais Neuf
	1791 Ransacked during the Revolution
	19th century Stripped of paneling and damaged
COMMISSIONED BY	The Avignon Popes
ARCHITECTS	Pierre Poisson of Mirepoix (Palais Vieux or Old Palace); Jean de Louvres (Palais Neuf or New Palace)
MATERIALS	Stone
STYLE	Medieval Gothic fortress

The Papal complex now belongs to the city of Avignon. The task of preservation is constantly underway. The frescoes in the Great Audience Hall by the 14th century artist Matteo Giovanetti have been meticulously restored, as are a series of exquisite 17th and 19th century Gobelin tapestries in the banqueting hall.

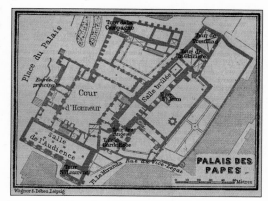

Crenellated battlements and machicolations protected the sumptuous palaces.

Facing page:
Façade of the fortified Palais Des Papes, home of the Avignon Popes in the 14th century.

Pierrefonds
Paris
FRANCE

Château de Pierrefonds

The picturesque Château de Pierrefonds stands on a promonotory in the marshy lands of Oise. It was part of the former county of Valois that belonged to Louis de Valois, Duc d'Orléans, brother and rival of king Charles VI. In 1390, Louis appointed Jean Lenoir to oversee the construction of a grandiose castle. In the early 16th century, the château was besieged and taken by royal forces, as its castellan supported the revolt of the Prince of Condé. It was partially dismantled and left to ruin until purchased by Napoleon I around 1810. It soon became fashionable at the royal court as a 'romantic ruin', and in 1857, Napoleon III asked Eugène Viollet-le-Duc to undertake its restoration at the cost of several million francs. The work carried on until 1885 with considerable enthusiasm, and a somewhat imaginative though not entirely accurate reconstruction of the château interior. Its exterior, however, retains most of its original military design.

In keeping with the style of 14th century medieval fortifications, Pierrefonds has a nearly symmetrical plan. Its rectangular high curtain wall is guarded by round angle towers. There are further towers at the center of each side; the largest one on the south side shields the main gateway. A moat and a defensive outwork provide another layer of protection at the entry point. Interestingly, the towers and the wall are at the same height, and a machicolated parapet runs the entire perimeter of the fortification, accessed by a covered wall walk. The garrison barracks and lodging for the ducal retainers were ranged along the inside walls, and the impressive multi-storied ducal residence was placed near the main gateway.

The wall of Pierrefonds are the same height as the round angle towers. Note the covered wall walk with machicolations encircling the top perimeter of the keep.

ADDRESS	xxxxxxxxx
CONSTRUCTION PERIOD	**1390–1407** Construction of towered enceinte wall, outer works and separating moat
	Early 17th century Castle partly dismantled; roofs destroyed; walls and towers damaged
	1857 Restoration and rebuilding
COMMISSIONED BY	Louis d'Orleans, Duke of Valois
ARCHITECTS	Jean Lenoir (14th century); Eugène Viollet-le-Duc (19th century)
MATERIALS	Stone
STYLE	Château

The monument was opened to the public in 1867. With its white stone walls, grey roof turrets and crenellated battlements, Pierrefonds is an elegant romantic castle. Among its highlights are the covered parapet walk and the grand imperial apartments.

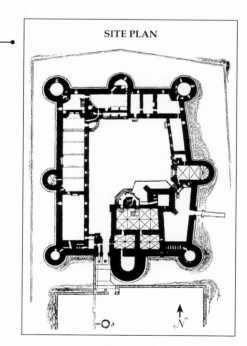

SITE PLAN

Facing page:
Pierrefonds castle was a favored ducal residence in the late Middle Ages.

The inner courtyard with the regal entrance to the restored ducal apartments.

Château de Tarascon

Situated on the grey rocks on the east bank of the Rhône river this imposing castle is reminiscent of the Bastille in Paris. Located 14 miles from Avignon, the town and castle are named after the mythological monster Tarasque, a dragon-like creature that terrorized the region in ancient times. According to legend, it was tamed and brought to the town by St Martha, an event that led to many of the townspeople converting to Christianity. The present castle was begun in the late 14th century by Louis II of Anjou, Count of Provence, and finished by his second son, René I of Naples, which is why it is locally referred to as King René's Castle. Tarascon reverted to the Crown in 1481, and was used as a prison till 1926.

Viewed from the opposite bank, the castle conveys an impression of strength and permanence. The flanking towers and curtain wall are the same height, while the main tower rises to 157.5ft (48m). Machicolated battlements line the walls, and the wider roof platforms provided a greater mobility for defending troops. An arched bridge leads over the moat into the first courtyard, which in turn leads into the second courtyard or the *Court'honneur*. This was the main residential section, with the royal apartments, chapel and galleries. Here the château appears lighter and more graceful, with mullioned windows, arched galleries and dressed stone decorations that reflect a high degree of medieval comfort and grandeur. A spiral staircase leads to the upper floors.

ADDRESS	Château de Tarascon, Boulevard de Roi Rene, 13150 Tarascon, France
CONSTRUCTION PERIOD	15th century
COMMISSIONED BY	Counts of Provence
MATERIALS	Stone
STYLE	Late medieval château

The Château was acquired by the state in 1932 and has been since restored and opened to visitors. The inner courtyard has busts of King René and his second wife Jeanne of Naval. On the opposite bank of the river is the 12th century donjon of Beaucare.

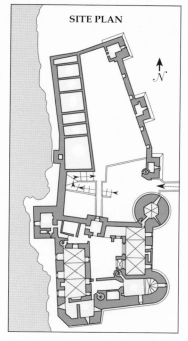

SITE PLAN

N

Crenellated battlements run along the walls and towers, and the glass windows had iron bars for security.

The gardens inside the castle walls.

Facing page:
The high-walled Tarascon castle is situated along the banks of the Rhone in southern France. Locally known as King Renés Castle, it blended a simple exterior with an appropriately regal interior.

FRANCE

Paris

Bonaguil

Château de Bonaguil

Bonaguil means 'bonne aiguilles' or 'good needle', referring perhaps to the needle-shaped narrow hill on which this château is perched in a picturesque valley in south-west France. Originally built as a narrow keep by Arnaud la Tour de Fumel in the 13th century, it eventually transformed into an almost perfect artillery castle. In its final form Bonaguil is considered a predecessor to Vauban's forts of the 16th century.

The Fumel's support for the English in the Hundred Years War led to constant warfare and left the castle in ruins, which then eventually passed to the Roquefeuil family, who enlarged and modifed it. By the 17th century, the château and the family fortunes had both declined. It was purchased and restored in 1761 by Marguerite de Fumel. Following the revolution of 1789, Bonaguil was declared as *bien national* (national property), and stripped of its valuables, roofing, paneling and even the floors. It was purchased by the Commune of Fumel in 1860.

The original polygonal keep was expanded in the late 15th century by Jean de Roquefeuille, but it was his son Berenger who conceived the notion of redesigning the castle as an artillery stronghold. Somewhat delusional, he lived in fear of constant attack, and spent a fortune gearing up the castle to meet it. A barbican and six new towers were added with low gun loops, and a *caponiere* was set up in the moat to sweep it clean of the enemy. He built vaulted casemated passages and an enormous buttressed artillery terrace. The corbels in the castle walkways were strengthened to take the weight of guns. Ironically, none of this was put to the test as Bonaguil was never attacked.

A view of the Lot valley from the highest point of the castle.

ADDRESS	Bonaguil Castle, Town Hall Fumel, 47 500 Fumel
CONSTRUCTION HISTORY	**1259–71** Polygonal keep and courtyard; palisade wall
	1337–1453 Destroyed in the Hundred Years War.
	1470–82 Additions to the keep
	1483–1510 Towers added with low gun loops; high round tower barbican; caponiere;
	1761 West esplanade; apartments refurbished
	20th century Phased restoration
COMMISSIONED BY	The Fumel and Roquefeuil families
MATERIALS	Stone
STYLE	Bailey and keep, artilley fort

Bonaguil drew praise from the well-known traveler Lawrence of Arabia, who visited it in 1908 and commented that "it is so perfect that it is ridiculous to call it a ruin." Illuminated at night, it hosts an annual music event and a spectacular fireworks show. A popular attraction is the medieval graffiti on the castle walls.

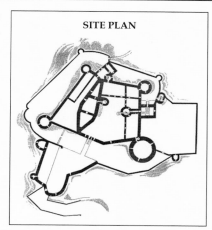
SITE PLAN

Facing page:
The tall towers and keep at Bonaguil castle are encircled by strong artillery fortifications built by Jean de Rocquefille in the 15th century. They were never put to the test, and later reduced to create terraced spaces.

Sunlight pours in from a delicately tinted glass window of the castle.

GERMANY

Berlin

Wartburg

Wartburg Castle

Wartburg castle sits on a steep ridge above the town of Eisenach in the Erfurt region of Germany. It was founded by Ludwig van der Schauenburg in 1076, and was the home of the powerful Thuringian Landgrave family for 200 years. Wealthy, cultured and ambitious, the Landgraves built an impressive Romanesque citadel as their primary residence. Legend has it that they held an annual 'Minnesinger' or Minstrel's contest at the castle, which later featured in Richard Wagner's 19th century opera *Tannhäuser*. Elizabeth of Hungary (later St Elizabeth) lived here as the bride of Count Ludwig IV. She was highly regarded for her charity and devotion and canonized after her death in 1231.

Wartburg was witness to momentous events in German history. In 1521, Martin Luther took refuge here, and prepared the first translation of the Bible into German. In October 1817, 500 students gathered for the Wartburgfest, the first ever student demonstration in Germany, that raised the cry for a unified nation, 'Honor, Freedom and Fatherland!'

Buildings were added throughout the middle ages and show a mix of Gothic, Romanesque and Renaissance styles. The well-preserved 12th century Romanesque palace is perhaps the oldest structure, and contains the Festsaal (main hall) with frescoes by Motitz von Schwind. The other buildings include the half-timbered Knights Hall, the Elizabeth Hallway, the gatehouse and the main tower.

ADDRESS	Wartburg 99817 Eisenach, Germany
CONSTRUCTION HISTORY	**1080** Timbered structure with two towers
	1317 Fire; new chapel and Palace
	14th–16th century Extensive additions
	1838–90 Rebuilding and renovation by Duke Alexander of Saxe-Weimar-Eisenach, with the assistance of architect Hugo von Ritgen.
	1952–54 Restoration by East German government
COMMISSIONED BY	Ludwig van der Schauenburg; Counts of Thuringia
MATERIALS	Wood, stone
STYLE	Hill castle; Gothic, Romanesque

Wartburg has been restored in phases from the 19th century. In 1922, the management of the castle was taken over by Wartburg Foundation. Luther's room is still preserved, and the castle museum contains a host of medieval art treasures, including reliquaries, paintings by Lucas Cranach the Elder, and the famous Dürer cupboard.

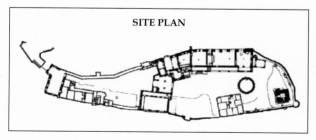

SITE PLAN

Facing page:
An interesting mix of styles are seen in the various buildings at Wartburg Castle. The tall watchtower is the oldest part of the complex.

The buildings of the inner castle, with timber detailing.

Martin Luther's study is still preserved at the castle.

GERMANY

Berlin

Marksburg

Marksburg Castle

The Rhineland is studded with castles, built in an age when the river Rhine was the main means of transporting men and material through the heartland of Germany. In the turbulent days of the Holy Roman Empire, numerous German barons built their strongholds on rocky spurs and outcrops along the spectacular valleys of this swift-flowing river. Marksburg is one of best preserved of these medieval castles, located on a hill above the pleasant town of Braubach, in the valley of Loreley. Perhaps built around 1177 by a local nobleman, it is first mentioned in local records in 1231. Its Rhine toll was established in the mid-13th century, around which time Count Eberhard II of Eppstein built its triangular keep. By 1479, Marksburg was turned into a gun fortress by the Landgraves of Hesse. In 1803 the Duchy of Nassau used the castle as a prison, and in 1866, it was ceded to Prussia after the Austro-Prussian War. In 1900, Marksburg was purchased by the German Castles Association for a 1000 gold marks.

Three ranges of buildings surround the 13th-century tower and triangular courtyard. The architecture is a mix of several styles-- there is a Romanesque Hall on the north side with superbly crafted windows, and a Gothic Great Hall on the eastern side. The chapel of St Mark, with fine painted walls and ceilings, occupies the southern corner. Battlements, covered passages, and gun bastions were added to the castle's defenses over the centuries. Marksburg was the only Rhenish stronghold that was not taken during the Thirty Years' War in the 17th century.

ADDRESS	Marksburg 56338 Braubach
CONSTRUCTION PERIOD	**1177** First structures
	1200-1250s Square tower or bergfried, triangular keep; Romanesque Great Hall
	14th century Chapel of St Marks; outer line of defenses
	Late 15th century Gothic Great Hall, bedchambers and banqueting hall; additions to tower
	Late 15th–18th century Gun batteries; round towers and wall
COMMISSIONED BY	Count Eberhard II of Eppstein
MATERIALS	Stone and timber
STYLE	Bergfried castle; Romanesque, Gothic

Marksburg is the administrative headquarters of the German Castles Association, dedicated to the preservation of the Rhine castles along the 40 mile (65 km) stretch of the upper and middle valley.

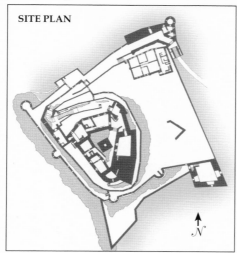

SITE PLAN

Facing page:
The original tower rises high above the surrounding buildings in the Rhine castle of Marksburg.

The white-washed walls of the tower keep within the castle walls.

Painted ceiling of the Chapel of St Marks.

GERMANY

Berlin

Eltz

Burg Eltz

Located on a rock spur high above the forests of Rhineland-Pfalz, near Wierschem, the impressive Burg Eltz is bounded on three sides by the Eltzbach River. On the fourth side a narrow road winds up the steep slope to the castle entrance. Eltz is a perfect example of a 'ganerbenburg', which refers to the German tradition of a castle shared by joint heirs of the same family. It came into the possession of the Counts of Eltz in the 12th century, and by 1268, various branches of the family had settled into six different *häusers* or houses around the semi-circular courtyard. The buildings were extensively rebuilt in the 15th century, and at present, there exist three main *häusers* of the Rübenach, Rodendorf and Kempenich families. In 1815, Graf Hugo Philipp became the sole owner of the castle, and extensive repairs were carried out during 1845-88.

The earliest structure is the Pflaz-Eltz tower, followed by the 14th century chapel. The remaining buildings, totally numbering over a 100 rooms, are constructed cheek-by-jowl in a mix of decorative styles and functions. The walls rise to eight floors, turrets abound everywhere, and bartizans project out from the upper stories. The Rübenach and Rodendorf *häusers* are Gothic masterpieces, with massive oak beams, decorative woodwork, fireplaces, elegant tapestries, wall frescoes and paintings. The Elector's room in the Rodendorf House displays an outstanding Flemish tapestry depicting a hunting scene. A rare painting by Lucas Cranach the Elder, *Madonna with Child and Grapes*, can be seen in the Rübenach Lower Hall, where the Gothic fireplace has a cast iron plate manufactured in the Eiffel in 1537.

Numerous buildings open into the narrow streets of the castle.

ADDRESS	xxxxxxx
CONSTRUCTION HISTORY	**12th century** The Pflaz-Eltz tower
	Mid-13th–14th century Chapel; several *häusers* of the different branches of the family
	1472 Rübenach house completed
	1490–1540 Rodendorf house completed
	1530 Kempenich houses completed
COMMISSIONED BY	The Eltz family
MATERIALS	Stone and timber
STYLE	Rock castle, ganerbenburg

Thirty-three generations of the family have resided in Burg Eltz for the past 800 years. At present, the castle is privately maintained by its owner, Dr Karl Graf von und zu Eltz. All the rooms are open to the public, except the Kempenich *häuser*, which is the family's private area.

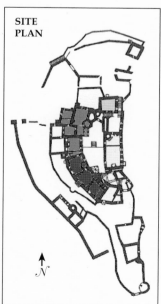

SITE PLAN

N

Facing page:
The quintessential family residence, Burg Eltz presents a dramatic picture, with its high walls and conical turrets framed against the green forests of the Rhine valley.

Tightly-packed buildings with different architectural features.

GERMANY

Berlin

Heidelberg

Heidelberg Castle

Rising to a height of over 300 ft (90 m) above the Necker river, the imposing Heidelberg castle was the stronghold of the Palatine princes who ruled in southern Germany from the 13th to the 17th century. First references to the castle date to 1303, and subsequent centuries saw it expanded to an upper and lower castle, with several-storied palaces and gardens in an eclectic mix of German Gothic, Renaissance and Baroque styles.

Heidelberg was devastated by wars in the 17th and 18th centuries. The famous Palatinate library was carried off to the Vatican by the Imperial army in 1623, and French forces wrought havoc in 1689 and 1693. The castle was abandoned in 1720 when the court moved to Mannheim. A lightning strike caused severe damage in 1764, and for a time the castle was reduced to a quarry for building material for the townspeople. In the early 19th century, restoration work began on the initiative of a French Count, Charles Graf von Graimberg, who began to guard and document the collections at the castle. Around 1900, the interiors of the Friedrich Building were restored, but a large part of the castle complex is in ruins even today.

ADDRESS	Schlosshof 69117 Heidelberg, Germany
CONSTRUCTION HISTORY	**14th century** Upper and lower castle
	1554 The upper castle destroyed by a lightning strike
	1556–59 Elector Ottoheinrich's builds lavishly decorated Renaissance palace
	1610 Freidrich Building and Palace gardens built by Elector Frederick V, who also commissioned the Elizabeth Gate in honor of his Stuart bride
	1622 Imperial troops sack Heidelberg
	1685–93 French destroy Heidelberg in the War of the Palatine Succession
	1764 Lightning strike
	1810–present day Restoration of interiors
COMMISSIONED BY	Electors of Palatine
MATERIALS	Red sandstone
STYLE	Hill castle; German Gothic, Renaissance and Baroque

The Administration of the State-Owned Palaces and Gardens of Baden-Württemberg is responsible for Heidelberg Palace. The popular Heidelberg Festival is held in the castle every year. The cellar of the Friedrich Building contains the Heidelberg Tun, a gigantic wine vat dating to 1751 with a capacity of 49,000 gallons (185,500 litres).

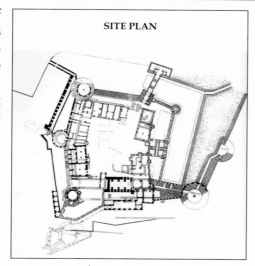

SITE PLAN

Through the centuries, Heidelberg has been damaged by war, lightning and fire.

The Heidelburg Tun ,a giant wine barrel, stands 55 ft (7 m) high, and has a dance floor on top.

Facing page:
Heidelberg castle stands in ruined splendor on the northern side of the Königstuhl hill.

GERMANY

Berlin

Pfalzgrafenstein

Pfalzgrafenstein

The most unusually located of the Rhenish castles, Plafzgrafenstein sits on a rocky island in the upper Rhine river. It is a region of thickly forested valleys and turbulent history. The writer Victor Hugo described the castle as a "ship in stone, eternally afloat upon the Rhine." Its prow faced upstream, and it was one of the many toll castles or bergs built by the Princes of Bavaria to control the prosperous trade along this major artery. It acted as a customs station in conjunction with the adjacent castle of Gutenfels, located on a higher point on the right side of the Rhine, making it well nigh impossible for boats to escape the toll. The Pflaz Island also served as a river crossing point for General Blucher's army of 60,000, in their hot pursuit of Napoleon in the winter of 1814. Toll collection ceased in 1866, when the berg was acquired by Prussia, and in 1946, ownership passed to the State of Rheinland-Pflaz.

The oldest structure in the castle is the tall pentagonal tower erected by Ludwig of Bavaria in the 14th century. The hexagonal curtain wall and corner turrets were built a little later. Some additions were made in the 16th century to accommodate an artillery bastion, and a characteristic baroque cap was probably added to the keep in the late 17th century.

ADDRESS	xxxxx
CONSTRUCTION HISTORY	**1327** Pentagonal-shaped keep or *bergfried* in a courtyard
	1338–42 Hexagonal curtain wall (12 m ? ft) with defensive passageway and corner turrets
	1600s Gun bastion facing upstream and reinforcing defensive passageway
	1760s Baroque roof on keep
COMMISSIONED BY	Ludwig of Bavaria
STYLE	Island castle; Baroque

The Pflaz is now a carefully restored museum, with its interiors as spartan as they were in the high Middle Ages. Special attention has been paid to the Baroque details in the restoration. It is linked to the shore by a river ferry from the town of Kaub, located on the banks below Gutenfels.

Plafzgrafenstein forms part of the UNESCO World Heritage Site 'Upper Middle Rhine Valley', a 65-km (40 miles) stretch of the Rhine valley with historic castles, towns and vineyards.

Facing page:
Plafzgrafenstein resembles a ship in full steam, its prow turned upstream. This unusually sited castle was an important toll station along the river, and there was a chain stretched across the waters to stop any defaulters.

A view of the neat façade, with white washed walls with red trim.

Interior galleries with wooden railings overlook the castle yard.

GREECE

Athens

Rhodes

Rhodes Castle

Exceedingly strong and a marvel of military engineering, Rhodes Castle was the unassailable command center of the Knights Hospitaller, a wealthy brotherhood of medieval military knights. After the fall of Acre heralded the end of the Crusades, the Order conquered the Byzantine held island of Rhodes in 1309, and set up a new base in the Mediterranean. The existing castle was rebuilt, and a well-defended port with two adjacent harbors was established. Under Grandmaster Pierre d'Aubusson, Rhodes Castle withstood a historic and bloody siege by the Ottoman army in 1479–80. Nine of its towers and the Grandmaster's Palace were destroyed, but the fort held on. However, the Turks returned in force in 1522, with a fleet of 400 ships and wore down the defenders after a six-month siege. The Italians occupied Rhodes in 1912, when the Grandmaster's Palace was refurbished as a luxurious summer residence for King Victor Emmanuel III.

The castle walls with its square towers enclose the town, and they were of exceptional thickness and height. A second lower wall was built alongside to protect the base of the outer wall, and polygonal bulwarks were added in the 15th century. The entire length of the curtain was machicolated, and divided into sectors, which were allotted to different *tongues* or nationalities of knights. The Grandmasters Palace and arsenal were located near the Post of Germany and the Post of France, while the Post of England defended the other end of the wall, adjacent to the merchant's quarter. The gallery port was defended by the circular Tower of St Nicola, which was a small castle in itself with external fortifications and mounted cannon. The commercial port was protected by the towers of St Naillac and St Agnelo, which faced each other across the harbor opening.

Front façade of the Grandmaster's Palace.

ADDRESS	T K 85100, Rhodes, Rhodes (Prefecture of Dodekanissa), Greece
CONSTRUCTION HISTORY	**11th–13th century** Byzantine citadel with several towers and church
	14th century Wall and square towers; Grandmasters Palace
	1361 Tower of St Nicolas
	1436 Tower of St Agnelo
	1450 External bulwarks
	19th century Post-Renaissance renovation of Grandmaster's Palace
COMMISSIONED BY	Knights Hospitaller
MATERIALS	Stone
STYLE	Fortified town, citadel; Byzantine, Gothic, Renaissance

In 1948, Rhodes became part of Greece. The entire complex of the old castle, with its squares, various churches (some converted to mosques), the imposing Knight's Hospital and residences of the knights, is open to the public. It also contains the famous Rhodes Archaeological Museum.

Facing page:
The headquarters of the Knights Hospitaller in the 14th century, Rhodes castle faced its toughest challenge from the Turks in the 15th and 16th century.

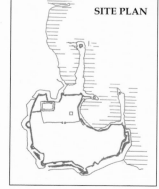

SITE PLAN

A section of the external wall.

Salgo

Budapest

HUNGARY

Salgo Castle

Salgo Castle is located on a basalt ridge at a height of 2050 ft (625 m) above the village of Salgóbánya, 75 miles (120 km) from Budapest. The Kacsics clan controlled the area in the 13th century, and built a high tower on this location to guard against the Mongol threat. Around 1460, King Matthias granted the estate to the nobleman Imre Szapolyai, who expanded and strengthed the fortress. During the Turkish invasion of Hungary in the 1520s, Salgo was heavily besieged and reduced to a shell by consistent artillery fire. Over the following centuries, it was inherited by several prominent families, including the famous Hunagarian poet Bálint Balassi, but the castle remained in a generally ruined state until modern times.

The original fortification consisted of a square stone tower with a small bailey. The outer bailey was built in the 15th century, when the inner yard was roofed over to become the castellan's residence. The water supply on this high location was organized through two cisterns. A pentagonal battlement was built on the east side in the 16th century.

Staircase leading up to the tower.

ADDRESS	3100 Salgótarján, Salgóbánya, Hungary
CONSTRUCTION HISTORY	**1240s** Stone tower; inner ward; water cisterns
	1450s Outer yard with stables and storehouses; inner yard roofed as castellan's residence
	16th century Battlement for artillery
COMMISSIONED BY	Lords of Salgótarján
MATERIALS	Stone
STYLE	Rock castle; Tower keep and bailey

Salgo castle is state-owned, and under the management of the Treasury Property Directorate. Archeological and restoration work in the fortress has been in process since 1998, and the stone tower has been reconstructed and roofed.

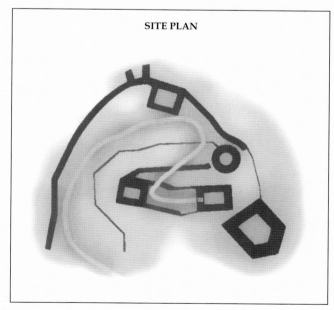

SITE PLAN

The Castle affords a magnificent view of the surrounding country.

Facing page:
Located on a high ridge, Salgo Castle withstood the invasions of the Hussites and the Turks in the Middle Ages. It is now partially restored.

Visegrad
Budapest
HUNGARY

Visegrad Castle

Located atop a hill on a bend of the Danube River, the 13th-century medieval fortress of Viségrad is actually a complex of several structures. It comprises of the high citadel at the top of the hill, the lower castle with the Solomon's Tower, and a royal palace in the town below. King Bela IV began construction of the castle in 1247, as part of a general surge of fortification after the fearsome Mongol invasions of Hungary in 1241. In 1323, Charles I of the Angevin dynasty moved his court to Viségrad, where he hosted the celebrated Royal Summit of Kings between the Czech, Hungarian and Polish monarchs. During his time the Hungarian coronation insignia and the Polish Crown Jewels were kept in Viségrad. The town developed into a prosperous trade center, and remained politically significant until the Turkish conquest in the 15th century. Legend has it that around 1460, Vlad Tepes of Wallachia, later known as Count Dracula, was imprisoned for a time at Viségrad. After the liberation of Buda in 1686, Viségrad was successfully besieged by the Austrians, and the castle heavily damaged. It was left in a ruined state until reconstruction work began in 1871.

The citadel, originally a triangular fort with two towers, commands a breathtaking view of the countryside and the river Danube. It also served as a customs house, and the road passed right through the castle yard. The five-story Solomon's Tower was used as a residence and is one of the best examples of Romanesque construction in Central Europe. It was connected by a wall to the upper citadel.

A sumptuous royal palace on the lower slopes is also included in the royal complex of Viségrad. It was begun by Charles I, and extended by Sigismund of Luxembourg in the late 14th century. However, it was transformed into an elegant edifice in the 15th century by King Matthias Corvinus and Queen Beatrice, the daughter of the king of Naples. Elegant marble fountains and stone carvings graced its halls and terraces in the best traditions of the early Italian Renaissance.

ADDRESS	Viségrad, Pest, Hungary
CONSTRUCTION HISTORY	**1240s** Triangular upper castle with two towers
	14th–15th century New wings and external walls
	15th century Renaissance palace
	Early 18th century Destroyed in battle with Austrian army
	19th–20th century Reconstruction and restoration
COMMISSIONED BY	Bela IV of Hungary
MATERIALS	Stone
STYLE	Keep and bailey castle; Romanesque (tower), Renaissance (palace)

The citadel and the restored palace now house the Viségrad Museum.

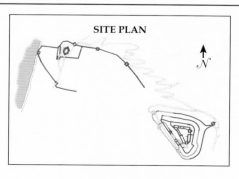

SITE PLAN

N

Facing page:
The fortification at Viségrad consisted of an upper and lower castle, connected by a wall.

Solomon's Tower.

A portion of the upper castle. In the distance is the path leading to the citadel.

New Delhi

INDIA

Chittaurgarh

Chittorgarh

The largest fortified complex in India, Chittor was the ancient capital of the region of Mewar, ruled by the Sisodia Rajput clans from the eighth century. It was besieged several times, and the tales of its fiercely independent and proud defenders have passed into local legend. In 1303, the sultan of Delhi, Aladudin Khalji, laid siege to the castle. Faced with an implacable foe, the queen and all the women of the castle committed *jauhar* or immolation by fire, while the men led a suicidal charge into the enemy's ranks. Chittor was conquered again in 1535 by the sultan of Gujarat. In 1568, it faced its last major siege, when it was surrounded by the Mughal army commanded by the emperor Akbar. It was abandoned afterwards, and when the Sisodias regained their lands in the 17th century, they shifted their capital to Udaipur.

The fort sits astride an elevated ridge and covers an area of 690 acres (280 ha). A battlemented wall punctuated by fortified gateways encloses the vast inner ground, which contains several palaces, temples, gardens, 22 water tanks, as well as garrison quarters, fields and hutments. From the river at the base of the hill, a path winds steeply upwards, through several *pols* or gateways, to reach the main entranceway called Ram Pol. The palaces are built in stone, with rooms arranged around public and private courtyards. Exquisite canopied windows and pavilions grace the buildings, and gardens and summer palaces were built around the major water bodies. Among them is the three-storied Padmini's palace in the middle of a small lake. An eight-story Victory Tower was erected by Rana Kumbha (*r*.1433–68), to commemorate his victory over the sultan of Malwa in 1440. It is intricately carved with figurative, floral and geometric motifs. Such lavish decoration is also visible in the temples, particularly the jewel-like Meera Temple, built for the 16th-century ascetic queen of Mewar, who is revered today as a poet-saint.

ADDRESS	Chittor fort, Chittor district, Rajasthan, India
CONSTRUCTION HISTORY	8th–15th century Fort walls, gateways; Rana Kumbha's palace
	12th century Kirti Stambha (FameTower)
	1440 Jai Stambha (Victory Tower)
	19th century Reconstruction of Padmini's Palace
COMMISSIONED BY	Ranas of Mewar
MATERIALS	Sandstone
STYLE	Fortified town and citadel; medieval Indian

The entire complex is under the management of the Archeological Survey of India. It is open to the public, and a son et lumière show is available in the winter season.

SITE PLAN

Facing page:
A view of Rana Kumbha's palace within the castle, which was the main royal residence. Its canopied windows are typical of medieval Hindu architecture.

The massive fortifications of Chittor are largely intact.

The eight-story Jai Stambha or Victory Tower is the highest structure in the fort.

New Delhi

Kumbhalgarh

INDIA

Kumbhalgarh

The remote fortress of Kumbhalgarh is located atop a steep ridge of the Aravalli hills, 50 miles (80 km) west of the city of Udaipur. It was one of the numerous forts built by Rana Kumbha (r.1433–68), the energetic 15th-century ruler of the kingdom of Mewar (southwest Rajasthan), and served as the refuge of the royal family in times of crisis. Around 1535, the infant Rana Udai Singh survived an assassination attempt, and was raised in anonymity at Kumbhalgarh before returning to the capital at Chittor to claim his kingdom. In 1568, Chittor was sacked by the Mughal army under the command of Emperor Akbar. Faced with certain defeat, Rana Pratap retreated to the virtually inaccessible citadel at Kumbhalgarh to continue a bitter and long-drawn struggle against the Mughals, that lasted over a century.

A long crenellated outer wall interspersed with watchtowers and rounded bastions created an extensive protected perimeter in the surrounding hills, while the citadel itself was protected by two further walls to create a 'fort within a fort'. The main gateway is flanked by massive, rounded towers. This leads to a steep, twisted passageway which goes past temples, barracks and domestic ranges to reach the Badal Mahal (or Palace of the Clouds) right at the summit of the castle. The interiors at Kumbhalgarh are somewhat austere, but all the structures are impressive for their sheer strength and majesty. Within the palaces, rooms are arranged around courtyards, and narrow staircases lead to first floor chambers and roof terraces. Several water tanks, farmland and a village also existed within the fort walls.

Two rounded towers protect the entrance gate of Kumbhalgarh, called the Ram Pol.

ADDRESS	Kumbhalgarh, P.O. Kelwara, District Rajsamand, Rajasthan
CONSTRUCTION HISTORY	**1580s** First construction
	1800s Expanded with many new buildings
COMMISSIONED BY	Rana Kumbha of Mewar
MATERIALS	Stone
STYLE	Concentric rock castle; Medieval Indian

Prayers are still offered at the temples within the castle, which are the shrines of the clan and family deities of the Ranas of Mewar. The castle is under the management of the Archeological Survey of India, and is open to the public.

Facing page:
The king's palace at the summit of the castle offers panoramic views of the surrounding forested Aravalli hills. The walls of Kumbhalgarh extend over 22 miles (36 km).

A ribbed exterior dome in the Badal Mahal (Palace of the Clouds) topped by a gilded finial.

New Delhi

INDIA

Golconda

Golconda Castle

The medieval kingdom of Golconda (in the modern state of Andhra Pradesh) owed much of its prosperity to the diamond trade. The nearby diamond mines produced many famous diamonds, including the legendary Koh-i-noor. In the 16th century, Golconda was ruled by the Qutb Shahi dynasty who built a formidable citadel on a granite hill, five miles (eight km) from present day Hyderabad. It is considered one of the best examples of medieval fortification in India. Designed to withstand the armies of the Mughals, it was gradually expanded over generations to achieve its present imposing dimensions. The fortress remained virtually impregnable until 1687, when it was attacked by the Mughal emperor Aurangzeb, and was forced to yield after a nine-month siege.

The outer perimeter wall had eight gateways. These had enormous doors set with metal spikes to deter enemy elephants from battering them in. The inner citadel was located at the highest point on the eastern side, and protected by a double wall. The approach to the castle was deliberately twisted, and flanked by steep walls and the rock face. An amazing acoustic feature of the castle is that a hand clap under the domed Fateh Darwaza (or Victory Gate) at the outer wall, could be heard at the Bala Hisar, which is the highest point of the castle nearly half a mile away.

Within the enormous enclosure are palaces, pavilions, gardens, domestic buildings, and soldier's quarters. The walls are battlemented with provision for artillery, and a complex system of cisterns ensured a supply of water. The graceful domes, arched colonnades, wall decorations, and carefully planned gardens are typical of the evolving Hindu-Islamic architecture of the time.

ADDRESS	Opposite Army Quarters, Golconda, Hyderabad - 500008
CONSTRUCTION HISTORY	16th century
COMMISSIONED BY	Qutb Shahi sultans
MATERIALS	Granite
STYLE	Concentric castle; medieval Indian (Deccan)

Golconda Fort is open to the public, and a son et lumière show brings alive its history for visitors. It is managed by the Archeological Survey of India, which is also responsible for its restoration. A mosque is located near the summit of the citadel.

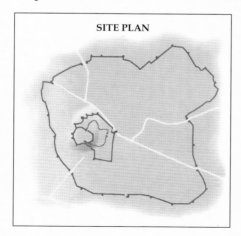

SITE PLAN

Facing page:
The spacious complex of Golconda fort reflected the prosperity of the kingdom, which derived large revenues from the diamond trade.

Natural rock formations and man-made walls provide layers of protection within the castle walls.

Typical arched galleries around a courtyard in one of the castle buildings.

IRELAND

Dublin

Blarney

Blarney Castle

Situated six miles northwest of Cork, Blarney castle dates back to a wooden hunting lodge in the 10th century. The first stone structure came up around 1210, and the present battlemented keep was the work of Dermot McCarthy in 1446. The castle was taken by the parliamentarians in 1646, but given back to the McCarthy family after the Restoration. However they forfeited the estate after the Williamite Wars in which they supported James II. It was purchased by Sir James St. John Jefferyes, the Governor of Cork in 1688. The new owners built a Georgian residence adjacent to the keep, and laid out a landscaped rock garden. A fire destroyed the house in 1820, and it was replaced in 1874 by Blarney House, a grand Scottish-style baronial mansion.

Situated high on the battlements of the keep is the famous Blarney stone. It is supposed to be a portion of the legendary Stone of Sconce of Scotland, given to Cormac McCarthy by Robert Bruce for support in the Battle of Bannockburn in 1314. The stone is said to reward anyone who kisses it with the gift of eloquence. Those desiring to kiss the stone must lean outwards from the parapet over the machicolations, a daring feat performed by hundreds of visitors everyday. Blarney's association with expressive speech is also attributed to an incident in the 16th century when the castellan Cormac Teige McCarthy was supposed to affirm his allegiance to Queen Elizabeth I. Reluctant to submit, he delayed the inevitable by sending numerous long-winded epistles which were dismissed by the exasperated queen as 'a lot of Blarney'.

The moss-covered inner walls of Blarney keep.

ADDRESS	Blarney Castle, Blarney, County Cork, Ireland
CONSTRUCTION PERIOD	13th to 14th century
	10th century wooden lodge
	c. 1210 stone fortress
	1446 battlemented square tower and bailey
	18th century Mansion and rock garden
	1820 fire damages residence
	1874 new baronial mansion
COMMISSIONED BY	Dermot McCarthy
MATERIALS	Limestone
STYLE	Stone keep and bailey

Blarney Castle is a popular destination, and much of its fame rests on its promise of 'the gift of the gab'. Besides the keep and mansion, there are extensive gardens and rock formations, which have imaginative names such as *Druid's circle, Wishing steps* and *Witch's cave.*

Facing page:
The high stone keep of Blarney castle with machicolated battlements is surrounded by it ruined wall and towers.

Kissing the Blarney stone is supposed to grant the gift of eloquence, for which the Irish are justly famous.

IRELAND

Dublin

Dublin Castle

Dublin Castle served as the seat of colonial administration from the Norman conquest of Ireland in 1169 till the end of the English rule in 1922. During this time it was also the official residence of the Lord Lieutenant or Viceroy, a records office, a state prison, the royal treasury and an armaments store.

The 13th century fortress ordered by King John occupied the highest ridge in the area, and was an example of a 'keepless' fort with a strong encircling wall and four massive drum towers at the corners. It was bounded by the river Poddle and an artificial moat. All that remains of the original structure today is the Records office tower, as a devastating fire in 1684 destroyed the medieval timber buildings in the castle bailey. Major reconstruction over the next century resulted in the splendid edifices in the Upper and Lower Yard, including the glorious State Apartments with their impressive Georgian interiors. Notable here are the Throne room, and St. Patrick's Hall with its 18th century allegorical ceiling paintings by Vincenzo Valdre. The Chapel Royal is a Neo-Gothic structure with 100 heads carved out of limestone.

After Henry VIII broke with Rome, Ireland became a battleground between the Irish Catholic and the English, with Dublin at the centre of the storm. Those supporting the English were often derided as 'Castle Catholics'. The Statue of Justice guarding the castle entrance from Cork Hill was seen by the cynical as 'turning its back' on Dubliners. In 1907, the Crown jewels of Ireland were stolen from the Bedford Tower and never recovered. Since the establishment of the Irish Free State in 1922, many state ceremonials continue to be held within the castle, though it is no longer an administrative center. In 1938, Douglas Hyde was inaugurated as the President of Ireland in Dublin Castle, setting a precedent that has been since followed. The remarkable Chester Beatty library and the Gallery of Modern Art are housed in Bermingham Tower.

ADDRESS	2 Palace Street, Co. Dublin Castle, Dublin 2, Ireland
CONSTRUCTION PERIOD	1204–28; 17th to 18th century
	10th century Viking fortress
	1170's Norman wood and stone castle
	1204–28 Stone fortification with surrounding moat and towers, no central keep
	1684 Major fire destroys buildings and most of the castle
	18th century Major reconstruction; Upper and Lower Yard, State apartments, offices and towers, barracks and stables
COMMISSIONED BY	King John
MATERIALS	Stone, timber
STYLE	Norman, Georgian

Dublin Castle is under the management of the Office of Public Works. After recent refurbishment, it is also a major conference centre, and hosted part of the European Council in 2004.

Facing page:
A mix of archtitectural syles at Dublin castle: seen here is the Round Tower dating to Norman times, and the Georgian structures of the 18th century.

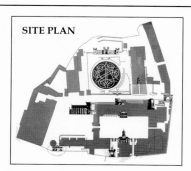
SITE PLAN

The Bedford Tower of 1761 in the Georgian courtyard, flanked by the gates of Fortitude and Justice. It was from here that the Crown Jewels of Ireland were stolen in 1907.

The lavishly appointed State Drawing Room in the State Apartments.

Trim Castle

Trim castle in County Meath is the largest castle in the country. Located on the banks of the river Boyne, it stood at the very edge of the Pale — the enclave of Norman occupation at the eastern edge of Ireland — and consequently, at the brink of battle through most of the Middle Ages. The Norman lord Hugh de Lacy was granted the estate of Meath by King Henry II, but the ringwork that he built in 1173 was razed to ground in a year by the Irish. It was rebuilt very soon, as a 13th-century Irish chronicle *The Song of Dermot and the Earl* mentions a massive keep at Trim. The castle then passed to the Genneville and then the Mortimer family, before devolving to the English Crown in 1461. It served as an administrative seat and mint, and was refortified in the Cromwellian Wars in the 1640s. It was granted to the Wellesley family in the 1680s, and finally acquired by the state in 1993.

The enormous three-story keep is built on a cruciform plan, with square towers projecting out from a central square. The first and second floors of the keep are divided by a cross wall, but the third floor, which is possibly of a later date, is a single chamber. This may have been the lord's private apartment. The chapel was in the eastern tower, and mural passages led to the different levels in the keep. The surrounding bailey is of a triangular shape, enclosed by a curtain wall, punctuated by mural towers and two gatehouses — the Dublin gate in the south, and the Trim gate in the west. The latter has remnants of an earlier wooden gate. Most of the walls near the river front have vanished, as has the north tower of the keep.

The walls and grounds of the castle.

ADDRESS	Trim, Co Meath
CONSTRUCTION HISTORY	**1173** Motte and keep
	1174 Keep destroyed and motte leveled
	c. 1190–1240 Square keep; triangular bailey with square mural towers; gatehouse
	13th–16th century Domestic ranges; stables; renovations and additions to the keep; tower on northern corner of curtain.
	Late 20th century to date Restoration
COMMISSIONED BY	Norman lords of Meath
MATERIALS	Stone
STYLE	Tower keep

At present, conservation work is in progress, but the castle is open to visitors.

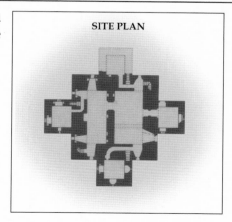
SITE PLAN

Facing page:
The redoubtable Trim castle was a key Norman stronghold in Ireland in the Middle Ages. The keep is built on a cruciform plan.

An entrance gateway.

NORTHERN
IRELAND

Carrickfergus

London

Carrickfergus Castle

From its vantage location on a rocky peninsula overlooking the entrance to Belfast slough, the imposing Carrickfergus castle controlled access to Belfast and the region of Ulster. It was built in the 13th century by the Norman adventurers John de Coucy and Hugh de Lacy, both intent on a private fiefdom in Ulster. King John captured the castle in 1210 and entrusted his constable de Serlane with the task of building a new curtain wall on a budget of £100. However, De Lacy recovered control in 1228. During Edward the Bruce's invasion of 1315–16, the Scots were able to take the town but not the castle. However the Earldom of Ulster declined in the years that followed, and Carrickfergus reverted to the crown in 1338. William III first set foot on Irish soil on 14th June 1690, at the quay below the castle, before proceeding to take Dublin and eventually win the historic Battle of the Boyne.

The castle is fairly small, and appears somewhat cramped. A narrow enceinte is set within a polygonal wall, containing a tall four-storey keep (90 ft high) as well as several other buildings and shelters. After 1228, De Lacy strengthened the castle walls with towers in the west and an imposing gateway on the north side.

The square castle keep with it crenellated battlements.

ADDRESS	Carrickfergus Castle, Marine Highway, Carrickfergus, BT38 7BG, UK
CONSTRUCTION PERIOD	12th century
	1180s to 1210 Inner ward and four storeys keep, polygonal wall
	1210 Outer wall along the rock face
	1228–42 Outer curtain wall with two polygonal towers in the west; twin towered gatehouse in the north with murder holes and portcullis
	16th century gatehouse towers reduced for artillery platforms
	1928 onwards restoration and exhibits
COMMISSIONED BY	John de Coucy and Hugh de Lacey
MATERIALS	Sandstone, basalt rubble (outer wall) and timber
STYLE	Concentric castle

Carrickfergus was used as a prison in 18th century, and served as a magazine and armory till 1928; cannons from the 18th and 19th century are on display at the castle. It is one of the best preserved medieval castles in Ireland, and is under the care of the Northern Ireland Environment Agency.

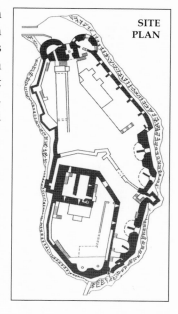

SITE PLAN

Gun port at the castle overlooking the harbour.

Facing page:
Its vantage location overlooking Belfast Slough made Carrickfergus indispensable to the control of Ulster.

Castel Sant' Angelo

This venerable landmark of Rome, capped by the shining statue of the Archangel Michael, is located on the right bank of the Tiber River. It is connected to the city by a handsome arched bridge. It originated around 135 CE as the family tomb of the Roman Emperor Publius Aelius Hadrian. By 400 CE, it had developed into a city fortification, and incorporated into the Aurelian city walls of Rome. The next hundred years of chaos saw it plundered by the Huns and the Goths. In 1084, the building became a refuge for the beleaguered Pope Gregory VII, during the bitterly fought Investiture dispute with the Holy Roman Emperor Henry IV. It survived a long drawn siege in 1527, and continued as a luxurious papal residence until the 17th century, after which it became a dreaded prison. In the famous third act of Giacumo Puccini's opera *Tosca*, the distraught heroine jumps to her death from the battlements of Castel Sant'Agnelo.

The original Roman structure was an imposing cylindrical edifice, which changed over time into a fortified urban castle. Pope Nicholas III (1277–80) built a covered passageway connecting the castel to St Peter's Basilica. Around 1400, Pope Boniface XI transformed the castel into a well-defended papal palace, with several floors containing residential chambers, a prison, and a storehouse. At the beginning of the 16th century, Pope Alexander VI commissioned Antonio da Sangallo to construct polygonal bastions and an outer wall.

According to legend, the Archangel Michael saved Rome from the plague in 950 CE, and in 1536, Raffaello da Montelupo created a marble statue of the guardian St Michael that was placed atop the castel. In 1753 it was replaced by a bronze statue made by the Flemish sculptor Peter Anton von Verschaffelt.

The illuminated Castel and bridge across the Tiber at night.

ADDRESS	Lungotevere Castello, 1, 00183 Roma, Italy
CONSTRUCTION HISTORY	*c.* **135 CE** Cylindrical tomb of Emperor Hadrian
	1277 Passetto di Borgo connecting to St Peter's
	*c.*1400 Papal palace
	c. **1470** Pope Nicholas V added round towers
	c. **1500** Polygonal bastions
COMMISSIONED BY	Emperor Hadrian (the tomb); Popes of Rome (the castel)
MATERIALS	Stone
STYLE	City castle; Gothic, Renaissance

Castel Sant'Angelo is now the Museo Nazionale de Castel Sant'Angelo, with a remarkable collection of art displayed over five floors.

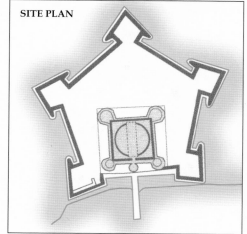

SITE PLAN

Facing page:
The cylindrical castle topped by the statue of St Michael is a landmark of Rome.

A statue of St Michael, the guardian of Rome, crowns the Castel Sant'Angelo.

Castel del Monte
ITALY
Rome

Castel del Monte

This highly atypical castle is situated in Andria in the Apulia region of southern Italy. It was the inspired creation of the Holy Roman Emperor Frederick II (*r.1220–50*), a monarch with unorthodox views and wide-ranging interests in science, art, and literature. Called *stupor mundi*, or 'wonder of the world', Frederick spoke six languages, and engaged in a long drawn out struggle with papal authority, even while journeying to the Holy Land to take part in the Fifth Crusade.

Castel del Monte, located on an elevation, is more a palace than a castle. Despite its imposing visage and extent, it does not appear to be geared up for battle and possibly served as a fortified hunting lodge. Octagonal in every aspect, the castle plan may have been inspired by Byzantine and Islamic architecture in the Near East, particularly the Dome of the Rock in Jerusalem. It has also been compared to the palace chapel at the Aachen cathedral, where Frederick had been crowned Emperor. Certainly, there is a recurring association with the number eight—the octagonal building has an octagonal courtyard and is surrounded by eight octagonal towers. There are eight rooms on each floor, the roofs of which are supported by ribbed vaulting. No expense was spared in the fine interiors of polished marble and polychrome mosaic, and there were even bathrooms with piped water. Taken as a whole, the Castel del Monte is an inspired blend of classical and Islamic elements in a stark Gothic mold.

ADDRESS	Via Castel Del Monte, 70031, Andria, Italy
CONSTRUCTION PERIOD	1240–50
COMMISSIONED BY	Frederick II, Holy Roman Emperor
MATERIALS	Stone
STYLE	Palace-castle; Gothic

Abandoned for centuries, the castle was gradually stripped of its marble and carved pillars by vandals and those looking for building material. The Italian government purchased it in 1876 ,and the process of restoration began in 1928. The Italian one Euro-cent coin displays the Castel del Monte on the reverse.

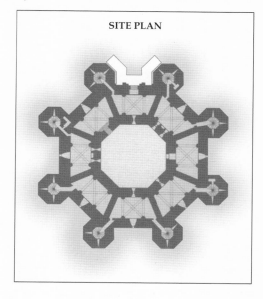

SITE PLAN

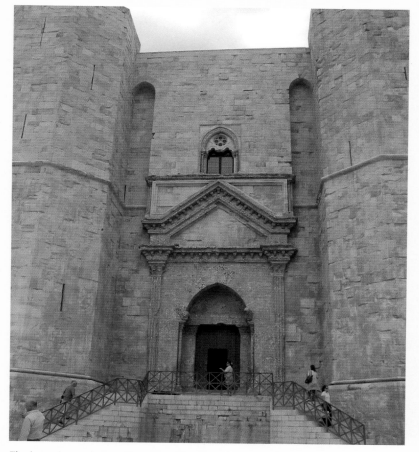

The imposing main entrance.

A window detail with an interesting mix of stone.

Facing page:
Frederick II's grand palace-castle was never intended to be defended in battle.

ITALY
Rome
Caetani

Castello Caetani

The town of Sermoneta dates back to Roman times, when it was a busy *entrepôt* along the coastal trade routes in the present-day Lazio region of central Italy. In the 13th century it developed into a fortified town dominated by a castle, which was controlled by the Anibaldi family. In 1297, the castle was acquired by the Caetani family, an illustrious name among the nobility of medieval Italy. They were dispossessed for a short time in 1497 when the Borgia Pope Alexander VI excommunicated the family and gave their castle to his nephew Rodrigo, son of his sister Lucrezia. However, Pope Julius II restored the castle to the Caetanis in 1504, and they continued to live in their ancestral property till 1977, when the family died out, and management was entrusted to the Caetani Foundation.

Excellently preserved, the massive Castello Caetani is an irregular quadrilateral in plan. The earliest structure is the large donjon in the south corner which dates to the 10th century. The residential chambers and banqueting hall are ranged around a courtyard, and were added after the 13th century. The Borgias expanded the fortifications with the assistance of Antonio Da Sangallo the Elder, a famous military engineer of medieval Italy. There are some exceptional 15th century murals in the main bedchambers.

ADDRESS	Castello Caetani di Sermoneta, Via della Fortezza - 04010 Sermoneta (LT)
CONSTRUCTION HISTORY	**10th century** Square donjon and curtain wall
	1297–1400 Expansion of domestic ranges; banqueting hall east of donjon
	1497–1504 Fortifications strengthened
	16–20th century Interiors gradually modernized; restoration and preservation efforts
COMMISSIONED BY	The Caetani family
MATERIALS	Stone
STYLE	Fortified town and castle

Some of the rooms contain noteworthy frescoes and some excellent medieval furniture. The adjoining Ninfa Gardens also form part of the castle estate and are managed by the Caetani Foundation. The castle is open to the public.

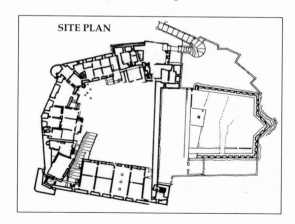

SITE PLAN

Facing page:
The Castello Caetani was owned by the same family for 700 years. Its massive ramparts enclose well-preserved medieval halls and a large tower.

Town dwellings are nestled along the castle walls.

A birds-eye view of the castello

ITALY

Rome

Naples

Castel Nuovo

The Castel Nuovo is a historic landmark of the coastal city of Naples, and formed part of a ring of protective castles in Campania in the Middle Ages. The original structure was called Maschio Angioino, or the Angevin Keep, as it was built in 1297 for Charles I of Anjou by Pierre d'Agincourt. Not much remains of this, as it was almost entirely rebuilt around the 1450s by Catalan architects on the instructions of Alfonso of Aragon. The new castle was called Castel Nuovo, and it became the main center of Neapolitan administration. In 1495, while in French hands, it was besieged by Spanish forces under the command of the famous General Gonsalvo of Cordoba, who detonated a mine of gunpowder under the castle barbican. Naples changed hands several times between the Spanish and the French, and the Castel remained in use as an occasional residence and a garrison headquarters until the 16th century.

An irregular rectangular enceinte is protected by five large drum towers. Four stand at the corners, and the fifth is at the mid-point of the smallest side, making a protected entranceway. An impressive double height triumphal arch was built between these two towers by Francesco Laurana around 1460 to welcome Alfonso V of Aragon. A second, much lower, outer curtain wall was added later for defensive artillery, and the moat provided another layer of protection. A multitude of rooms are placed around the courtyard, their function ranging from the mundane to the majestic.

ADDRESS	Piazza Municipio, Naples, Italy
CONSTRUCTION HISTORY	**1279–82** First castle keep and enceinte
	Mid–15th century Extensive rebuilding; triumphal arch, outer artillery bastion
	1823 restoration begins
COMMISSIONED BY	Charles I of Anjou
ARCHITECTS	Pierre d'Agincourt (13th century, Maschio Angioino) Francesco Laurana (15th century triumphal arch)
MATERIALS	Sandstone
STYLE	City castle; bailey with towers

The Castel del Nuovo is owned by the Commune of Naples. It houses the Neapolitan Society of National History, which has an extensive collection of rare manuscripts, prints and drawings. There is also a large collection of religious art works.

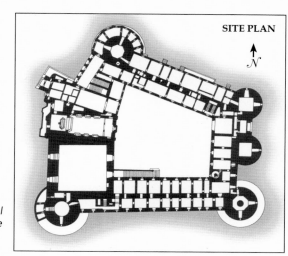

Facing page:
Though ruled by different dynasties in the Middle Ages, Castel Nuovo remained the main administrative center of Naples. The majestic triumphal archway between the entrance towers was built in the mid–15th century.

SITE PLAN

The massive ridged base of the corner drum towers.

The vaulted domed ceiling in the Baron's Hall.

ITALY
Volterra
Rome

Volterra Castle

Volterra's medieval castle complex is located at the crest of a hill in the beautiful region of Tuscany in northern Italy. The town below has ancient roots, and was a prosperous settlement in Etruscan and Roman times. In the early Middle Ages, it came under the rule of bishops of the Holy Roman Empire. The rise of local lords led to the building of the earliest fortification called the Rocca Vecchia (Old Castle) between 1292–1430. In 1472, the Medici lords of Florence conquered Volterra and Duke Lorenzo extended the castle to incorporate a formidable Rocca Nuova (New Castle).

The old and new structures are linked by a battlemented wall with a continuous walkway. This created a middle bailey between the two castles which could house a garrison or accommodate the townspeople in times of crisis. Interestingly, in local parlance, the central round tower of the Rocca Nuova is known as the Maschio (Male) while the semi-elliptical tower of the Rocca Vecchia as the Femmina (Female).

ADDRESS	Viale dei Ponti, 56048 Volterra (PI)
CONSTRUCTION HISTORY	**1292** Old Castle
	1340s Tower, outer walls and ditch
	1430 Outer wall extended
	1472–74 New Medici castle with circular main tower, rectangular bailey with round angle towers; double curtain wall to connect with Old Castle.
COMMISSIONED BY	Rulers of Volterra
MATERIALS	Stone
STYLE	Renaissance

The Volterra castle complex is well preserved. It is now a prison, and not open to the public.

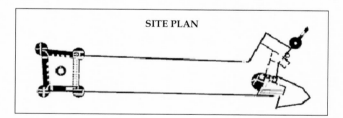

SITE PLAN

A view of the massive walls and towers.

Porta Fiorentina (1543), one of the gates in the town next to the castle.

Facing page:
Landscaped gardens surround the formidable bulk of Volterra castle, now a state prison.

ITALY

Verona

Rome

Castelvecchio

Castelvecchio (meaning 'old castle') in the north Italian town of Verona was built around 1350 by its autocratic ruler, Cangrande II della Scala. This compact yet stunning Gothic castle was intended as a deterrent to the rival city-states of Venice and Padua, and also to shelter the lords of Verona in the event of popular unrest against their autocratic rule. In 1404, after a brief period of confusion, Verona came under Venetian rule and the castle became a munitions store, and then the Venetian military academy. During Napoleon's occupation in 1797, it was the site of an anti-French revolt against forced conscription called the 'Pasque Veronesi'. In 1923, the castle was converted to a museum.

Castelvecchio has a square plan with seven towers and a high keep, situated adjacent to the river Adige. A moat surrounded the wall, and a fortified bridge led from the main entrance onto the main highway leading north. In the event of the castle being overtaken by their enemies, this was the escape route for the della Scalas into the domains of their traditional ally, the Holy Roman Empire. The structure is remarkably unadorned, except for the swallowtail merlons that run all along the perimeter wall and towers.

The pointed swallowtail merlons are the only adornment on the castle tower.

ADDRESS	Museo di Castelvecchio, Corso Castelvecchio, 2 Verona, Italy
CONSTRUCTION HISTORY	**1354–56** Castle and bridge
	1790s Barrack quarters
	1959–73 Restoration and renovation of museum
COMMISSIONED BY	Cangrande II della Scala
MATERIALS	Brick
STYLE	City castle; Gothic

During 1959–73, the castle was excellently restored by the architect Carlos Scarpa. It is now a state of the art museum displaying an enormous range of Italian art treasures, particularly of the Romanesque period. These include works by Andrea Mantegna, Jacopo Bellini and Pisanello, as well as ceramics, sculpture, gold objects and weaponry.

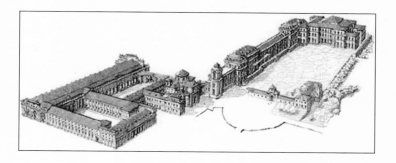

Facing page:
The beautifully illuminated Castelvecchio and the adjoining bridge across the river Adige.

An arched colonnade leading to the museum galleries.

JAPAN

Tokyo

Himeji •

Himeji Castle

The Himeji Castle complex in Hyogo prefecture epitomizes the best in Japanese defensive architecture of the medieval age, as it perfectly combines function with unparalleled grace and beauty. It is also known as the 'White Heron Castle' because of its brilliant white exterior. The site was first fortified in the 14th century, but a three-story tower came up in 1580. After the Battle of Sekigahara in 1600, the Tokugawa shogun Ieysasu granted Himeji to Ikeda Terumasa, who greatly expanded the castle. Much of what we see today dates to his time. Himeji was the last of the feudal strongholds to fall to the imperial army after the Meiji Restoration in 1868. It was auctioned off in 1871 for 23 yen.

The castle structures were built on platforms of rammed earth faced with large blocks of dressed stone. The walls consist of a framework of wood filled with bamboo and clay, the whole covered with plaster. The main keep, called the *tenshu*, is six stories high, each succeeding floor reducing in size from the one below. The traditional curved roofs have overhanging eaves with carved animals. The overhang rests on wooden beams, and the gap between the roof and wall could be used to drop missiles in a variation of European machicolations. Himeji castle has 11 gates and seven towers, and in additon to the main keep there are also three smaller *tenshu*. A maze of corridors and passages connect the different parts of the complex. These were deliberately designed to confuse intruders.

ADDRESS	68 Honmachi, Himeji-shi, Hyogo, Japan
CONSTRUCTION HISTORY	**1346** First castle
	c. **1580** Three-story keep
	1600–18 Fifty-acre complex of 86 buildings with main *tenshu*, additional *tenshu*, gateways and passages
	1956 Restoration begins
COMMISSIONED BY	Lords of Himeji
MATERIALS	Stone, wood, plaster, tile
STYLE	Keep and bailey; Medieval Japanese military

Himeji is the best surviving example of military architecture from the Shogunate era in the early 17th century. Despite being bombed twice, it miraculously escaped major damage in World War II. It is among the most visited sites in Japan, and also features in many movies and television series. A five-year restoration programme is underway, which will be completed in 2015.

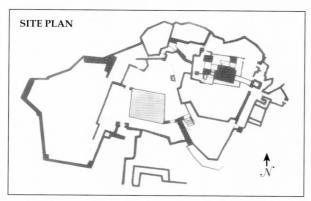

SITE PLAN

Facing page:
Himeji castle is an outstanding example of Japanese military architecture of the 17th century. The inhabitants were protected by man made rather than natural defenses.

Detail of roofs with overhanging eaves.

The interiors are fitted with wooden doors and windows in simple geometric lines.

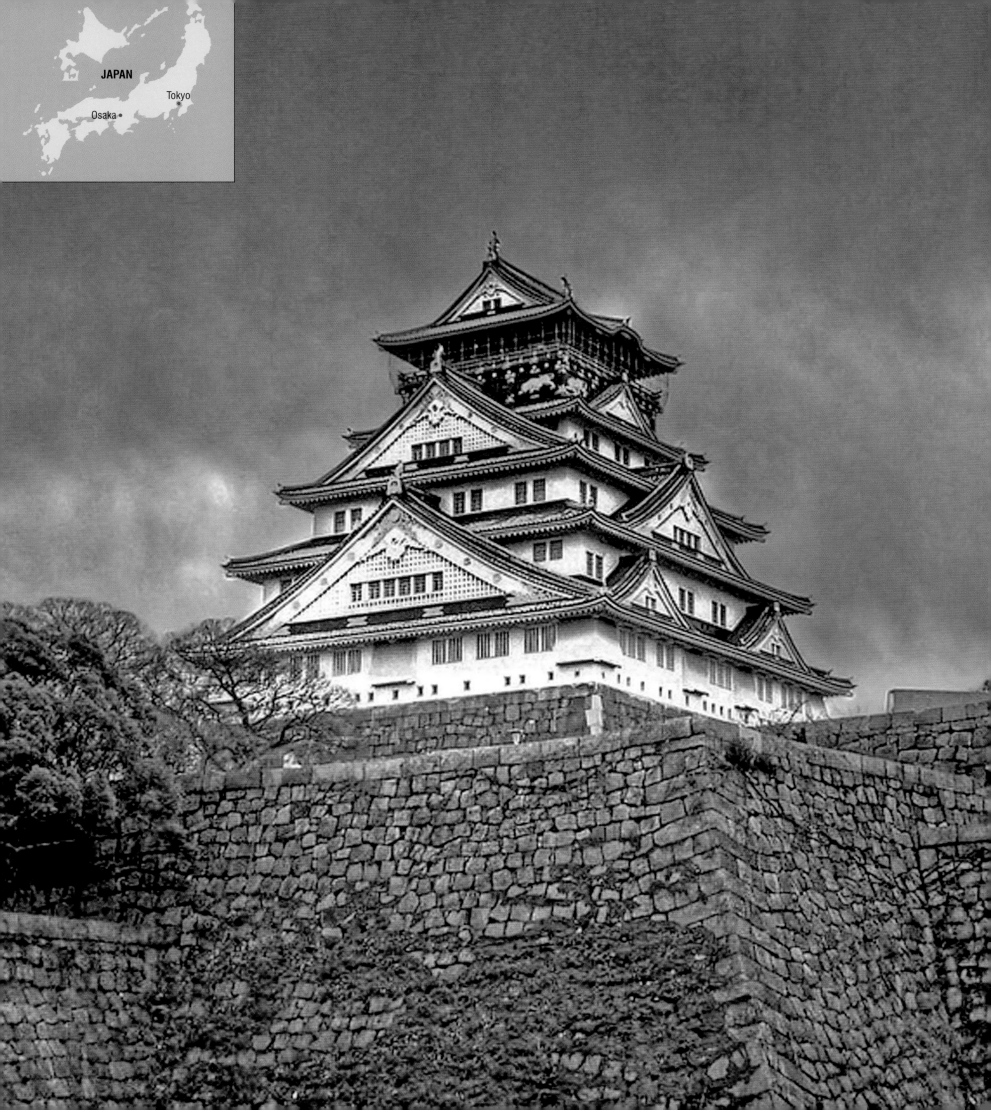

JAPAN

Tokyo

Osaka

Osaka Castle

One of the most famous castles in Japan, Osaka was first built in 1583 by the powerful lord Toyotomi Hideyoshi. A vast complex of gilded and decorated structures came up over 15 years, and construction was continued by his successor Toyotomo Hideyori. In 1603, the newly established Tokugawa Shogunate sought to curb rival *daimyos* or lords, including the Toyotomi clan. In 1614, Osaka was besieged by the vast army of Shogun Ieyasu, and its defendants sued for peace. The attackers withdrew after filling in the castle moats to render the castle defenseless. Within weeks, the Toyotomis began to dig up the moats again, and the shogun's army returned in full force. The Toyotomi forces were massacred and the castle destroyed. The shogun began a massive rebuilding in 1620, and the 64 western clans were each allocated a certain length of wall to build. The enormous blocks of stone used for this purpose were transported from quarries in the Inland Sea, and many are engraved with the elaborate crests of the various clans. Over the centuries, the castle tower was damaged by war, lightning, and finally, bombing in World War II.

Osaka relies on man-made rather than natural defenses, as was the custom with Japanese castles of this time. The castle is built on two raised platforms of landfill, surrounded by moats. The design was inspired by Azuchi Castle (1576), which was the first example of a tower keep in Japan. At Osaka, the main *tenshu* or keep is five stories on the outside, but also contains several underground floors. It is situated in an arrangement of baileys, passages and additional towers. The traditional curved roofs and white walls are embellished with golden roof tiles and carvings of fish, cranes and tigers. The original interiors were lavishly decorated. Included within the complex is a shrine to Toyotomi Hideyoshi.

ADDRESS	Osaka-jo, Chuo-ku, Osaka, Japan
CONSTRUCTION HISTORY	**1583** Construction begins of foundation and complex
	1585 Keep finished
	1597 Complex completed
	1615 Destroyed and burned
	1620–29 Rebuilt castle; five-story *tenshu*, new defenses
	1868 Castle damaged in war
	1928 Main *tenshu* restored
	1945 Bombed in World War II
	1995–97 Restored in concrete
COMMISSIONED BY	Toyotomi Hideyoshi
MATERIALS	Granite stone, wood, plaster, tiles
STYLE	Keep and bailey; Medieval Japanese military

The present castle is a ferro-concrete reproduction of the original. Osaka Castle and its extensive grounds are a major attraction, especially during festival days.

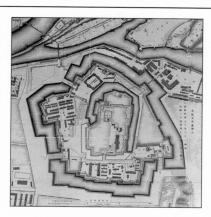

Facing page: A significant castle of medieval Japan, Osaka was rebuilt several times, and the present structure is a ferro-concrete reproduction of the 17th century original. Right: A 19th-century illustration of Osaka Castle.

Detail of the gilded and carved roof.

A shrine honoring the spot where Toyotomi Hideyori and his mother Yodo Dono committed ritual suicide on 14 June, 1615.

Riga **LATVIA**

Riga Castle

Riga Castle is the official residence of the President of Latvia, and some of its original oak foundations can be traced to the first castle towers built in the 14th century. At that time, the Livonian Order, a branch of the Teutonic Knights, defeated local resistance to set up a base in Riga. The townspeople were forced to construct a castle for the victors on the site of an existing Hospital of the Holy Ghost, on the banks of the river Daugava. Though the Rigans destroyed the castle again around 1484, they were bound by the Rules of Capitulation exacted by the Livonian overlords, and were compelled to reconstruct the castle. Riga passed through Lithuanian, Polish and Swedish hands, before coming under Russian hegemony in the early 18th century. It became the official residence of the President of the Republic of Latvia in 1922, and sustained heavy damage during World War II.

By 1515, Riga was a rectangular bailey with two round and two quadrangular towers, in diagonally opposite corners. A wide moat separated it from the city ramparts. The remarkably unostentatious exterior of the three-story structure may be due to the forced nature of its construction. The ground floor housed the guard quarters, kitchens and other functional rooms, while the upper floors contained the chambers of the Master of the Order, chapel, and various dining and meeting halls. A gallery looked down into the central courtyard. Gun bastions were added in the 16th century, while the interiors were remodeled throughout the 19th and 20th centuries.

The Presidential wing.

ADDRESS	Pils Square 3, Riga, LV 1900, Latvia
CONSTRUCTION HISTORY	**1330** wall and flanking towers
	1484 Castle destroyed
	1495–1515 Rebuilt; cannon towers
	17th century Rebuilding and expansion; arsenal
	1780s Court house
	1816 Gardens on the north side; Imperial rooms
	1939 Festival hall; Three-star tower; extensive remodeling
COMMISSIONED BY	Livonian Order of the Teutonic Knights
MATERIALS	Stone, timber
STYLE	City castle; bailey with towers

The Council of Latvian People Commissars occupied the castle in 1940–41. After the formation of the Latvian republic in 1995, it continued to be the offical residence of the Latvian president. It has several museums, including the Museum of Foreign Art, the Rainis Museum of Literature and Art History, and the Museum of History of Latvia.

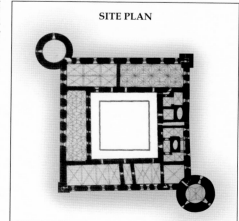

SITE PLAN

Facing page:
Riga castle on the banks of the Daugava River, has a simple exterior enlivened by elegant, tall spires.

A corner tower.

Gibelet (Byblos)

The present day city of Jubayl, located on the Mediterranean coast in Lebanon was known as Gebal to the Phoenicians, and Byblos to the Greeks. It is considered to be one of the oldest urban habitations, and was conquered around 1100 by the Crusaders, who named it Gibelet. They built a compact fortification in the town, and held it until 1188, when it was captured by Saladin. On his orders, some portions of the castle were dismantled. Within a decade it was retaken by Guy de Gilbert, who refortified the citadel. With the departure of the Crusaders, Gibelet was ruled by the Mameluk sultans, followed by the Ottomans.

This is a compact castle built of local limestone and building material culled from various ancient Roman edifices, which were in abundance in this historic region. Temple pillars were laid horizontally to strengthen the walls. The stone is en bosse, which is typical of Crusader masonry. The rectangular donjon is tightly enclosed by a curtain wall with square angle towers. There are two floors within with vaulted chambers. The entrance is from the north, through a gate tower, which was rebuilt by the Fatimids.

ADDRESS	Gibelet castle, Jubayl, Mount Lebanon Governate, Lebanon
CONSTRUCTION HISTORY	*c.* **1100** Square castle bailey; tower
	1188 Partial dismantling
	Early 12th century Refortified
COMMISSIONED BY	Crusader knights
MATERIALS	Limestone
STYLE	Tower keep and bailey

The castle was abandoned and left to ruin for many years. It is now an archeological site, open to the public.

Portions of a ruined tower.

The internal chambers.

Facing page:
The road leading to the castle ruins. Though built several times in history, not much remains of Byblos Castle today.

Sidon

The historic town of Sidon on the coast of Lebanon was captured by the Crusaders in 1111, and became one of the four lordships of the kingdom of Jerusalem. In 1187, Saladin conquered the town and dismantled the existing citadel. Around 1227, a group of Crusaders and pilgrims began construction of a sea castle on an island 325 ft (100 m) from the shore, that was connected to the mainland by a causeway. This fortification became an important garrison shelter for the Christian knights during the Saracen attacks in 1249, and the Mongol incursions of 1260.

The sea castle eventually devolved to the Order of the Knights Templar. They held it till the fall of Acre in 1291, when the Christian Crusades were finally abandoned. Shortly thereafter, it was dismantled on the order of the Mamluk sultans so as to discourage any attempts by the Crusaders to re-establish bases in the Holy Land.

All that exists now of this once impressive structure are two ruined towers joined by a wall. Remnants of Roman columns can be seen on the outer walls, which was in keeping with the Crusader custom of salvaging building material from nearby ancient sites. The Knights Templar probably added a covered shooting gallery and a vaulted hall.

ADDRESS	Kalaat Saida al-Bahriya, South Governate, Sidon District, Lebanon
CONSTRUCTION HISTORY	**1229** Construction begins
	1260s Additions by the Templars
	After 1291 Dismantled
COMMISSIONED BY	Crusader knights
MATERIALS	Stone
STYLE	Sea castle

The Sidon sea castle is open to the public. A popular three-day street carnival takes place annually on the stretch of highway adjacent to the castle.

A view from the harbor front of the ruined ramparts of the castle.

The castle is located on a natural island, linked to the shore by a arched causeway.

Facing page:
A valiant outpost of the Crusader knights, Sidon Castle saw many battles in the 13th century.

Vianden

LUXEMBOURG

Luxembourg

Château Vianden

The feudal castle-palace of the Counts of Vianden is located on an elevated rise in the Our valley, 25 miles north of Luxembourg. Remnants of a Roman fort and a Carolingian palace have been found at the site, but much of the construction dates to the 13th century, during the time of the influential Duke Henry I (1220–50). Nicknamed the 'Sun Count', he built a magnificent residence in keeping with the growing power and wealth of the house of Vianden. From 1417 to 1789, the castle was held by the Dukes of Nassau and Orange, and it was their principal home till 1530. Chateau Vianden came into the possession of King William I of Holland in 1820. He permitted it to be sold piecemeal, which reduced it to a near ruin.

A long path interrupted by three gates follows the base of the citadel to its main entranceway. The numerous palaces, towers and chapel within the complex are a marvel of Romanesque and Gothic architecture. The double oratory Romanesque chapel with a Gothic roof is dedicated to St Anthony. There is impressive Gothic vaulting in the Arms Hall and the magnificent Knights Hall—the latter could accommodate 500 men. Elegant Byzantine trefoil windows and a richly decorated Romanesque doorway can be seen in an upper gallery. The arms of Nassau and Orange are engraved on the keystones in the Arms Gallery.

ADDRESS	Château Vianden, BP 26, L-9401 Vianden, Luxembourg
CONSTRUCTION HISTORY	**5th century** Roman *castellum*
	9th century Carolingian palace
	11th century Square keep, chapel and hall
	12th–13th century Large palaces; chapel completed; Knights Hall; walls and gateways
	14th century *Quartier de Juliers* palace
	17th century House of Nassau, now in ruins
	1820's Dismantled piecemeal for building material
	1977 to date Rebuilding, restoration and preservation
COMMISSIONED BY	Counts of Vianden
MATERIALS	Slate and sandstone, timber
STYLE	Romanesque and Gothic

At its height, Vianden was one of the most impressive ducal residences in Europe. The writer Victor Hugo visited the castle in the 1860's and admired its beauty and fine interiors. It was extensively rebuilt after 1977, when its ownership passed to the State of Luxembourg. Today, it is managed by the foundation 'Les Amis du Château de Vianden'.

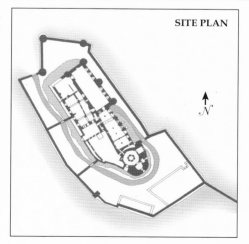

SITE PLAN

N

The corner tower at Vianden castle, with its sloping walls.

The elegant trefoil windows in the inner chambers of this famous ducal residence.

Facing page:
The redoubtable bulk of Vianden castle was the seat of the influential Dukes of Nassau and Orange from the 13th to the 16th century.

LITHUANIA

Vilnius

Trakai

Trakai

Located on an island in Lake Galvé, 17 miles (27 km) west of Vilnius, the castle of Trakai was of great strategic importance to the Grand Dukes of Lithuania in their struggle against the Teutonic Knights, in the 14th and 15th centuries. Probably begun around 1350 by Duke Kestatis, it was finished by 1409. After the Battle of Grunwald in 1410, when the Teutonic Knights were decisively defeated, it became the official seat of the Grand Dukes of Lithuania. When the ducal court moved to Vilnius in 1511, Trakai became a state prison. It was severely damaged in the Russian invasion of 1655, after which it faded into the background of national politics. Interest in its unusual architecture revived only with the Romantic revival of the 19th century.

Originally built of wood, the castle was eventually transformed into an unusual mix of stone at the lower levels, and brick on the upper floors. Timber was extensively used in the galleries and stairways. The architecture is mainly in the Gothic style, with the use of brick detailing in the windows and arches, and glazed tiles for the roofs. There are some excellent stained glass windows in the upper chambers of the donjon. A partial restoration project was undertaken by the Polish architect, J Borovskis, from 1929–41, but major reconstruction took place from 1962–87.

ADDRESS	Kestucio Str. 4, LT - 21004 Trakai
CONSTRUCTION HISTORY	**1350–1409** *Phase I:* basic U-shaped fortification, two distinct areas of the dukes residence and garrison quarters; *Phase II:* Three-story donjon at northern end, and outer wall extended; *Phase III:* moat separating two enceintes, gatehouse, defensive wall and towers added to lords bailey.
COMMISSIONED BY	Grand Dukes of Lithuania
MATERIALS	Stone (lower level) and brick (upper level)
STYLE	Island castle, wall, bailey and central keep

The island castle of Trakai is a proud symbol of Lithuanian national history, and it attracts scores of visitors each year. The Trakai History Museum is housed here, and its annual calendar includes many concerts, festivals and family events.

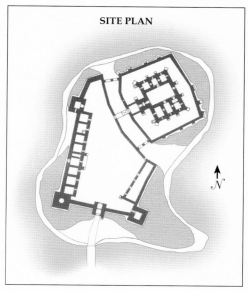

SITE PLAN

Facing page:
Trakai was a key castle in the defense of Lithuania against the mighty order of the Teutonic Knights in the Middle Ages.

The entrance to a main tower.

The lower levels are constructed of stone, while brick was used in the upper levels.

Muiderslot Castle

This excellently preserved moated brick castle derives its name from the Dutch word '*muiden*' which means 'mouth', referring to its location at the mouth of the river Vecht, nine miles (15 km) east of Amsterdam. This was an ideal spot from which to control the lucrative trade route to Utrecht, and the first castle was built in 1280 by Count Floris V, primarily as a fortified toll station. Shortly afterwards he was assassinated in the castle by rebellious nobles, and the structure demolished. What exists today is the brick castle built upon the older foundations by Albert of Bavaria, between 1370–86. In the 17th century, Pieter Corneliszoon Hooft (1581–1647), a writer and historian, was appointed Sheriff of Muiden and made the castle his home. He was a leading luminary of the Dutch Golden Age and founder of the *Muiderkring* or literary school of thought. Hooft invited many well-known artists, poets and playwrights to spend summers at the castle. By the 18th century, Muiderslot was derelict, and remained so until its restoration in modern times.

Roughly square in plan, Muiderslot is not large, though its brick walls are nearly five feet (1.5 m) thick, and it is well-defended by round corner towers and a machicolated gatehouse. The castle is sited in a substantial moat, and a covered wall walk runs the entire length of the wall.

ADDRESS	Muiderslot, Herengracht 1, 1398 AA Muiden, Netherlands
CONSTRUCTION HISTORY	**1000** Fortifications existed
	1280 Rebuilt and destroyed
	1370–86 Square moated bailey, machicolated gatehouse; covered wall walk, domestic range and Hall along the inside curtain wall, on the north and east.
COMMISSIONED BY	Count Floris V (13th century), Albert of Bavaria (14th century)
MATERIALS	Brick
STYLE	Moated castle

The castle houses the Rijksmuseum, and there is also on display an interesting collection of arms and armor. Muiderslot is managed by the Foundation Museum Muiderslot.

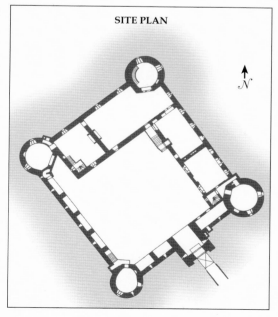

SITE PLAN

N

The castle courtyard.

Sculpture of Pieter Corneliszoon Hooft (1581–1647), sheriff of Muider Castle who was a prominent figure in the Golden Age of the Dutch Renaissance.

Facing page:
Muiderslot is a perfect example of a moated brick castle. It is set within a tranquil lake near the mouth of the river Vecht.

POLAND

•Marienburg

Warsaw

Marienburg Castle

Marienburg (now known as Malbork) is a classic example of a medieval Gothic brick castle. In the mid-13th century, the pagan lands of Prussia were conquered by the powerful Teutonic Knights, a fiercely zealous German Catholic order. In 1274, they began construction of a formidable stronghold on a piece of flat land by the Nogat River, 25 miles (40 km) from Gdansk in present day Poland. Marienburg became the capital of the order in 1309, and by 1407, the Teutonic Knights were at the height of their territorial power in the Baltic region. However, a Polish-Lithuanian military alliance decimated the Order's ranks in the battle of Tannenburg, and moved their forces on to besiege Marienburg. The castle held out under the leadership of Heinrich von Plausen, though the surrounding city was burned. Finally taken in 1457, it became a Polish royal residence, until then part of the newly created kingdom of Prussia in 1772. In the 1930s, the castle was a symbolic rallying point for Nazi propaganda, representing Germanic valor and strength. It was used as a prison in World War II.

As with all Teutonic castles, Marienburg served both monks and knights. It was divided into three distinct areas. The earliest to be built was the square Hochschloss (High Castle) with corner turrets, containing within it the chapel, chapter house, refectory, archives and warehouse. The Mittelschloss (Middle Castle) to the north contained the splendid palace of the Grandmasters (later the residence of the Polish king), the impressive vaulted refectories, the offices, arsenal and armor stores, and the guesthouses. Both the High and the Middle castles were surrounded by a moat. The forecastle in front of the Mittelschloss included the stables, barracks, armories and workshops. The castle's exterior fortifications eventually connected with the town walls.

The inner yard of the castle.

ADDRESS	Muzeum Zamkowe w Malborku, ul. Starościńska 1, 82-200 Malbork
CONSTRUCTION HISTORY	**1272–1300** High Castle
	1310–1400 Middle Castle
	Early 14th century to 1447 Forecastle
	18–19th century Badly damaged in wars
	1880–1920 Restoration by architect Konrad Steibrecht
	1939–45 Half the castle burned and destroyed
	1962 to date Restoration
COMMISSIONED BY	The Knights of the Teutonic Order of Holy Mary in Jerusalem
MATERIALS	Brick, tile
STYLE	Concentric moated castle; Gothic

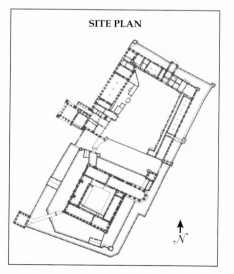

SITE PLAN

N

Restoration work began anew in 1962, and is still continuing. At present the castle has a museum with a son et lumière show.

Facing page:
The magnificent brick structure of Marienberg (Malbork Castle) was the Headquarters of the Teutonic Knights in the Middle Ages.

A vaulted ceiling in the interior.

Marienwerder

POLAND

Warsaw

Marienwerder Castle

The large red-brick castle of Marienwerder is located on the river Liwa, in Kwidzyn in northern Poland. The castle and town were founded by the military order of the Teutonic Knights around 1232, during their successful crusade in Prussia. Marienwerder is located just 24 miles (38 km) from their headquarters at Marienburg (Marlbok) castle, and it was also the seat of the influential Bishops of Pomerania. A splendid cathedral adjoins the castle, and it contains the tombs of many bishops as well as three Grandmasters of the Teutonic Knights. The power of the Order waned after 1407, and in 1466, Marienburg came under Polish rule. It eventually became part of the Kingdom of Prussia in 1701. The next two centuries saw many wars and changing owners, but in 1945, the town and castle of Marienwerder became part of Poland.

The castle and its attached cathedral dominate the surrounding town, and are a remarkable example of Gothic brick construction. The square Hochschloss or High Castle contains the Bishop's Palace and the convent house. The most remarkable feature of this castle is a high tower or *danske* with a stepped gable front, that served as a sewage tower. This tall square structure was separated from the main castle by a covered gallery bridge on five pointed arches. The cathedral has some magnificent painted frescos from the 14th century.

The castle forecourt.

ADDRESS	Kwidzyn, Poland
CONSTRUCTION HISTORY	14th century
	13th century Wooden castle
	1300–50 Brick fortification with bishop's palace; cathedral (1343–84); sewage tower
	1939–45 Badly damaged in World War II
COMMISSIONED BY	The Knights of the Teutonic Order of Holy Mary in Jerusalem
MATERIALS	Brick and tile
STYLE	Bailey castle; Gothic

Marienwerder was severely damaged during World War II, but has since been restored.

Above: The castle and cathedral at Marienwerder.
Facing page: The Teutonic Knights built enormous convent-castles in Poland, and were a dominant military power in the Baltic region during the Middle Ages.

The high tower or danske, separated from the main castle by a graceful arched bridge. Note the stepped gable fronts on the structures.

Guimarães

PORTUGAL

Lisbon

Guimarães Castle

National Monument

Located on a slight hill southeast of Braga (Minho), Guimarães castle occupies a special place in the history of Portugal as it is the birthplace of its first king Alonso Henrique in 1109. The infant's father was Henry of Burgundy, a younger son of the House of Burgundy, who came to seek his fortune in Spain in the late 11th century. He proved his mettle in the Reconquista campaigns of King Alonso VI of León. As a reward, Henry was married to the King's illegitimate daughter Teresa, Countess of Portugal, who brought the County of Portugal as her dowry. They established their court at Guimarães, building an enceinte around an existing 10th century tower. Alonso succeeded his father in 1112, and in 1139, after several years of warfare, declared his independence from León and took the title of King of Portugal.

Unusually for castles of this region, the central tower stands independent of the walls. A trapezoidal curtain wall contains four square corner towers. Entrances at the east and west walls are both flanked by twin gate towers. The crenellations running along the walls have pointed merlons, which are strongly indicative of Spain's Moorish heritage. Additions in the 15th century gave the castle its final form that is visible today.

ADDRESS	Rua Dona Teresa, Guimarães, Portugal
CONSTRUCTION HISTORY	**10–11th century** fortified tower; bailey and curtain wall
	15th century trapezoidal curtain wall with square towers, two sets of gatehouse towers
	1937–40 Restoration
COMMISSIONED BY	Henry, Count of Portugal
MATERIALS	Stone
STYLE	Tower keep and bailey castle

The castle narrowly escaped demolition in the 1830s. Today it enjoys the status of a national symbol. It was restored by the General Service for National Buildings and Monuments.

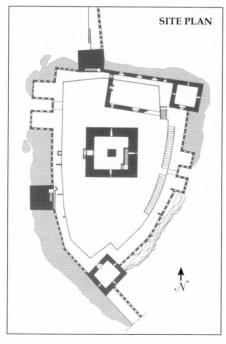

SITE PLAN

Facing page:
The original capital of the kingdom of Portugal, Guimarães is often called the 'Cradle of Portugal' as its first king, Alonso Henriques, was born here in 1109.

Detail of the interior buildings.

A section of the curtain wall with pointed merlons.

PORTUGAL

Leiria

Lisbon

Leiria Castle

The Romans had built a settlement in Leiria in ancient times, when the surrounding coastal region was an important trading area. The Moors established a fortification at the highest point overlooking the town in the 10th century. The first king of Portugal, Dom Alfonso Henriques, captured Leiria in 1135 as part of the Reconquista campaigns. However, it remained a disputed territory for the next seven years. The Moors retook it twice, and it was only in 1142 that Dom Alfonso could decisively establish his hold on the citadel. He and his successor rebuilt the walls and Leiria evolved into a significant royal domain. In 1254, Dom Alfonso III held the first form of Parliament or *Cortes* in Leiria.

It was a favored summer residence of King Dinis in the 15th century, who granted the castle as fief to his wife, Queen Isabel. He is credited with planting the famous *Pinhal de Leiria* (Pine forest of Leiria) in the surrounding coastal hills. The wood from these trees was used to build the Portuguese ships that explored the world in the 15th and 16th centuries.

The Moorish fort was considerably expanded and strengthened by the Portuguese kings. King John I built a Gothic palace with arched galleries that offer spectacular views of the surrounding landscape. He also rebuilt the Igreja de Nossa Senhora de Penha (Church of Our Lady of the Rock) located inside the castle.

ADDRESS	Leiria Castle, 2400 Leiria
CONSTRUCTION HISTORY	Roman site
	10th century Moorish fort
	12th century Rebuilt and refortified
	14th century Keep restored
	15th century Gothic royal palace;
	Church of Our Lady of the Rock rebuilt
COMMISSIONED BY	Kings of Portugal
MATERIALS	Stone
STYLE	Rock castle; Gothic

The castle is open to the public and parts of it are used to host exhibitions. The Gothic palace in the castle has been partially rebuilt.

Facing page:
Leiria was a favored royal residence of the Portuguese monarchy, and the site of the first cortes (parliament), in 1254.

A vaulted alcove in the castle interior.

The arched galleries in King John's palace provide sweeping views of the countryside.

PORTUGAL

Lisbon

Castello de São Jorge

The stern façade of the Castello de São Jorge has gazed down at the city of Lisbon for over 800 years. The Moors built the original *alcazaba* in the 10th century, when they controlled this prosperous trading town on the banks of the Tagus river. In 1147, the castello was wrested from them by the first king of Portugal Dom Alonso Henriques, after which Lisbon became a crucial base for the Christian Reconquista of Portugal. In 1255, Lisbon became the capital of Portugal and São Jorge was renovated as a royal residence. The castello was dedicated to St George by João I, perhaps out of respect for his English bride Phillipa of Lancaster. The national archives were housed in the *Torre do Tombo* or the Tower of the Archive from the 14th to the 16th century. The explorer Vasco de Gama was feted in the royal palace by King Manuel I in 1498, on his triumphal return from his voyages around the world.

From 1580, the Castello was used as a prison. It was severely damaged in an earthquake in 1755, and it remained neglected and in a state of general disrepair until a massive restoration program in the 1940s.

Rectangular in plan, the Castello boasts of a multitude of battlemented towers. Built around the earlier Moorish fort, its general appearance is stark, without much exterior embellishment. Within the walls are the remains of royal palaces, gardens and a large terraced square. It was partially protected by a moat and a low outer wall with a deep battered plinth.

ADDRESS	Rua de Santa Cruz do Castelo , 1100 Lisboa, Portugal
CONSTRUCTION HISTORY	**11th century** Moorish *alcazaba* or fortified citadel
	1197 Donjon added
	1300s Renovated
	1373–75 Construction of the walls of the castello and Lisbon city with a total of 18 towers
	1755 Earthquake damage
	1940s Extensive renovation
COMMISSIONED BY	Kings of Portugal
MATERIALS	Stone
STYLE	City castle; Gothic

The Castello de São Jorge has been at the center of Portugal's history, and is one of the foremost attractions in Lisbon

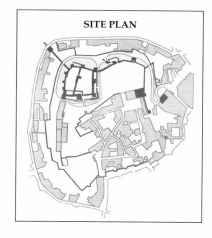

SITE PLAN

Facing page:
Square towers are placed at intervals along the long line of the castello's walls.

The wall walk along the battlements.

A statue of a Crusader knight at the castle.

ROMANIA
• Bran
• Bucharest

Bran Castle

This remote yet spectacular castle in Transylvania gained a mistaken notoriety as Dracula's Castle, after Bram Stoker made it the setting for his fictional tale of a vampire count. In fact, far from being a bloodthirsty monster, Vlad Tepes—the 15th century ruler of Wallachia on whom Stoker's character was based—is a national hero in Romania. He may have used Bran Castle as a base in his campaign against the Turks, but there is no clear evidence of it.

The first castle, built by the Teutonic Knights around 1212, was destroyed in the Mongol invasions thirty years later. In the 14th century, a new fortification was raised by the Saxon settlers of the nearby town of Brașov with permission from Louis I of Hungary (1342–82), for their own protection and to guard the trade route between Wallachia and Transylvania. Bran castle withstood the Turks in the late 14th century and continued to serve as a garrison fort and a customs point in the following centuries. It became a royal residence in 1920, occupied by Queen Marie and then her daughter Princess Ileana. After the communist takeover in 1948, the royal family was expelled, and the castle became state property. In 2006, the democratic government restored the castle to Princess Ileana's son, Dominic von Hapsburg.

The original fortification consisted of a high donjon and an enclosing wall. By the 16th century there was a round tower and gatehouse, as well as domestic buildings. Queen Marie made extensive renovations to modernize the castle with better water supply, heating and electricity. She refurbished the apartments and lavished care on the gardens and the estate.

ADDRESS	General Traian Mosoiu Street, No. 28, Bran, 507025 Brașov, Romania
CONSTRUCTION HISTORY	*c.* **1200** Wooden castle
	1241 Destroyed by Mongols
	14th century Stone donjon and wall
	15th–16th century Round tower, gatehouse, artillery works
	20th century to date Modern utilities, landscaping and interior renovations
COMMISSIONED BY	Teutonic Knights (1212); Saxons of Brașov (mid-13th century)
MATERIALS	Stone and wood
STYLE	Tower keep

Bran Castle is a major historical museum in Romania, managed jointly by the government and the von Hapsburg family. It is one of the most visited places in the country.

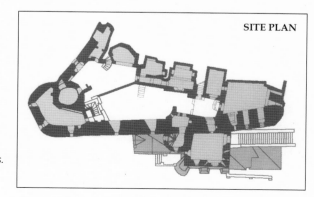

SITE PLAN

Facing page:
Though not very large, Bran resembles a storybook castle, with conical towers and red-tiled roofs. It was Queen Marie's favorite residence.

The interesting architectural features in the compact castle courtyard.

One of the beautifully kept interior apartments.

SCOTLAND

Edinburgh

London

Edinburgh Castle

Set atop a volcanic outcrop over 300 ft (90m) high, known as Castle Rock, Edinburgh castle dominates the skyline of the city below. Known in earlier times as Din Eidyn, it was first built in the reign of David I of Scotland in the 12th century. Though disrupted by constant warfare, the castle remained a royal residence till the Union of the Crowns in 1603. From the later part of the 17th century, it became a military base, with a large resident garrison.

Not many structures remain from before the 15th century save St Margaret's Chapel, built by David I, which is the oldest building in the citadel. In the 15th century, James III undertook a massive building program. His son, James IV, added the Great Hall with its hammerbeam roof, which is still used today for civic ceremonies and Hogmanay (New Year) celebrations. The other notable buildings around the Crown Square or courtyard, are the Royal Palace, and the Queen Anne building. The famous Half Moon battery is on the east side of the castle.

The most well-known treasure in the Crown Room of the Royal Palace is the Stone of Scone, the traditional throne on which the Kings of Scotland were crowned. It was removed to England by Edward I, and remained a bone of contention until returned to its rightful place in 1996.

ADDRESS	Castle Rock, Edinburgh, EH1, United Kingdom
CONSTRUCTION PERIOD	13th to the 15th century
	1130 fortress on Castle Rock
	15th century Extensive building; Great Hall
	1571–73 Destruction of David's Tower in the 'Lang Siege'
	1573–78 Reconstruction by Regent Morton; Half-moon battery
	19th century Gatehouse
COMMISSIONED BY	Kings of Scotland
MATERIALS	Stone and timber
STYLE	Rock castle

The castle is owned by the Ministry of Defense, and managed by Historic Scotland. The military presence is still visible through the Scottish National War Memorial and the National War Museum of Scotland located in the precincts. The annual Edinburgh Military Tattoo (part of the wider Edinburgh Festival) is held in the castle forecourt, called the Esplanade.

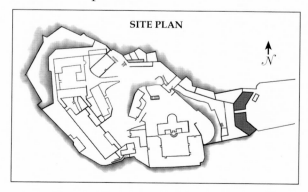

SITE PLAN

Facing page:
Edinburgh castle illuminated at night. The citadel is synonymous with Scottish pride and independence.

A cobblestone passage leads to up to the entrance.

Statue of Robert the Bruce ,the victor of the Battle of Bannockburn, at the castle entranceway.

SCOTLAND

• Caerlaverock

London

Caerlaverock Castle

Located in the Caerlaverock Nature Reserve, seven miles south of Dumfries, Caerlaverock castle was held for generations by the Maxwell chieftains. They traced their ancestry to Maccus, an 11th century warrior, after whom was named the barony of Maccuswell or Maxwell. Situated so close to the English border the castle was the site of many battles, and it was dismantled and rebuilt several times. In 1300, Edward I laid siege to Caerlaverock castle accompanied by 87 knights, a 1000 foot soldiers, and a new, giant trebuchet nicknamed the 'Warwolf'. Its deadly accuracy and Edward's subsequent victory were immortalized by contemporary poets, who sang of the coat-of arms and valiant deeds of the victorious knights. Just 13 years later, Eustace Maxwell supported Robert Bruce over Edward II, and dismantled the castle to reduce its importance to the English.

In 1640, the castle faced its last siege against the protestant Covenanters, who objected to the Maxwell support for the Catholic king Charles I. The garrison surrendered after 13 weeks, and the castle was stripped of its valuables. Its south curtain wall and tower were demolished, thus ending its life as a defensive edifice.

The first earthwork was abandoned in favor of a nearby elevated site, where a unique, triangular-shaped concentric castle was built in the 1280s. Surrounded by a deep wet moat, the castle was entered though an imposing two-towered gateway with machicolated battlements. The other two corners sported similar drum towers. A second line of defense was provided by high earthworks and a second moat. Over the centuries, living quarters were added to the gatehouse, and artillery ports constructed. Around 1630 Robert Maxwell, 1st Earl of Nithsdale built the splendid Nithsdale Lodging with its ornate Renaissance façade.

The massive twin-towered gateway.

ADDRESS	Glencaple, Dumfries and Galloway, Scotland, DG1 4RU, UK
CONSTRUCTION PERIOD	1280–90
	1230 Earthwork and timber fort
	1280s Stone concentric castle; towered gatehouse and drum towers, double line of moats separated by an earthwork.
	Early 14th century Castle dismantled
	15th century Gatehouse altered to create living areas
	16th century Gunports for artillery
	1630s Three-story guesthouse in a Renaissance style
	1640s captured and dismantled again
COMMISSIONED BY	Barons of Maxwell
MATERIALS	Stone and timber
STYLE	Concentric castle with moat

Caerlaverock is administered by Historic Scotland, which has put up a siege warfare exhibition and a children's adventure park.

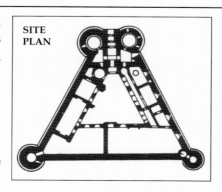

SITE PLAN

Facing page:
A corner tower of the triangular castle set within an idyllic moat. Note the machicolations atop the tower, and the ruined section beside it.

The Renaissance façade of the 17th century Nithsdale lodging contrasts sharply with the more sturdy stonework of the inner keep.

Eilan Donan

SCOTLAND

London

Eilean Donan Castle

This exquisite castle is easily one of the most photographed in the world, situated on an island at the juncture of three lakes — Loch Long, Loch Duich and Loch Alsh. The island and castle are named for Bishop Donnán who resided here in the 6th century. The original stronghold was built by Alexander II to guard against Viking invasions in the 12th century. By the late 13th century, the castle belonged to the MacKenzies of Kintail (later Earls of Seaforth), who dominated this patch of the Western Highlands and Isles. In 1511 they made the MacRaes hereditary constables of the castle.

In 1719, Eilean Donan was garrisoned by Spanish troops in an attempt to bolster the Jacobites rebellion. Three English Royal Navy frigates sailed into Loch Duich and forced the castle to surrender, after which it was destroyed with its own stock of gunpowder and subsequently abandoned.

Originally the castle perimeter extended around the island with a watch tower at the northern end. However, it became smaller in area over time, until it assumed its present shape of a compact, enclosed keep. With the advent of gunpowder in the 16th century, a horn work was added to create an octagonal firing bastion for cannon.

ADDRESS	Eilean Donan Castle, Dornie, by Kyle of Lochalsh IV40 8D
CONSTRUCTION PERIOD	13th century to 20th century
	13th century stone keep castle
	1719 destroyed by English warships
	1912–32 rebuilt and restored; a new bridge to the mainland
COMMISSIONED BY	Alexander II, Clan MacKenzie
MATERIALS	Stone and timber
STYLE	Rock castle, keep and curtain wall

It was bought in 1912 by Lt. Col John Macrae-Gilstrap, who spent the next two decades painstakingly restoring his ancestral home at a cost of £250,000. Today, Eilean Donan is managed by the Conchra Charitable Trust. Its spectacular location has made it a popular choice for film locations and weddings. Restoration work is still continuing, though major portions of the castle are available to the public.

Facing page:
The fairy-tale appearance of Eilean Donan castle gives no hint of its battle-scarred history. It was one of the strategic Scottish castles in the region of the Western Isles.

A poignant memorial in the castle keep honors the fallen heroes of the MacCrae clan during World War I.

One of the restored chambers within the keep.

Stirling Castle

The majestic Stirling castle was called the 'Key to Scotland', as it stood guard over the main crossing point of the river Forth, and thus the pass to the Highlands. Situated atop a steep ridge, the castle overlooks no less than seven famous battlefields. This includes the field of Bannockburn, where in 1314 Robert Bruce vanquished the English forces and avenged the ignominy of William Wallace's earlier defeat at Stirling Bridge in 1297. Often changing hands, Stirling was besieged countless times, the last being in 1746, when the Jacobites under Bonnie Prince Charlie tried and failed to take the castle. It was a favored residence of the Scottish monarchs, many of whom were born here.

It ceased to be a royal residence after the court moved to England in 1603, but continued as a garrison and its defenses were adapted to install gun batteries. From 1800 to 1964 the castle was a barracks and depot for the Argyll and Sutherland Highlanders.

From its humble origins as a 12th century earthwork fort, Stirling grew to become one of the best examples of Renaissance architecture in Scotland. Most of the structures that remain date to the 15th and 16th century, notable among them being the Great Hall (recently restored to its former glory) and the exquisite Chapel Royal with 17th century frescoes by Valentine Jenkins. The Royal Palace displays the Stirling Heads, roundels of wood of 38 figures, in Renaissance style, thought to be court luminaries of their day.

ADDRESS	Stirling Castle Esplanade, Stirling FK8 1EJ, UK
CONSTRUCTION PERIOD	12th -16th century
	Early 12th century earth and timber castle
	12th century walls and main structure, none of which remains today
	1490–1600 the King's Old Building, the Great Hall, central turreted gatehouse, curtain wall (James III); Royal Palace (James IV)
	1594 Chapel Royal rebuilt
	17th century frescoes in Chapel Royal
	1708 Grand Battery to site guns after the revolution of 1688
	1790 gun platform at Elphinstone Tower
COMMISSIONED BY	Kings of Scotland
MATERIALS	Stone, timber
STYLE	Renaissance

Stirling is a Scheduled Ancient Monument, managed by Historic Scotland. The Argyll and Sutherland Highlanders Museum is located within the castle in the King's Old Building. Restoration work continues, and a tapestry project is underway to recreate the 'Hunt of the Unicorn' tapestries in the Queens presence Chamber at the Royal Palace.

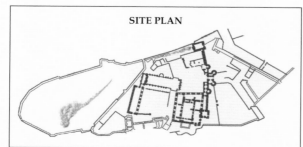

SITE PLAN

Facing page:
From its commanding height, Stirling dominated the politics of Scotland for three centuries.

The exterior façade of this historic castle. Note the stone detailing on the walls and windows.

A section of the 'Hunt of the Unicorn' tapestry.

SLOVAKIA

Spišský

Bratislava

UNESCO World Heritage Site

Originally a Hungarian border outpost, Spišský Hrad (or Spis Castle) eventually became one of the largest fortified complexes in Central Europe. It is located on a steep dolomite hill, and the first wooden structure to be built here was brought down in an earthquake in the 12th century. A stone castle, raised on the site by the 13th century, withstood the Mongol onslaught of 1240–42. Štefan Zápoľský, the wealthiest Hungarian noble in the 15th century, rebuilt the castle in a grand style, and his son Jan, a future king of Hungary, was born here in 1487. The hrad was later owned by the Turzo and the Csáky families.

Spišský Hrad contains all the elements of a classic castle with inner and outer walls, and several baileys. The upper castle or the inner bailey has the old circular keep, Knights Hall, the Romanesque palaces, the cistern and the chapel of St Elizabeth. The lower castle contains the administrative and other residential ranges, as well as the stables and barracks. The architecture is a mix of Gothic and Romanesque, and it is possible that Italian craftsmen were used in the palaces. Adapted to artilley, and also used as an arsenal, the castle suffered major damage in a fire in 1870.

ADDRESS	Víťaz-Dolina, Slovakia
CONSTRUCTION HISTORY	**12th century** Tower keep, wooden palisade; destroyed in earthquake
	13th century Stone castle and Romanesque palace
	14th century Lower castle
	15th century Upper castle rebuilt
	1780 Destroyed in fire
COMMISSIONED BY	Hungarian nobility
MATERIALS	Stone
STYLE	Rock castle; concentric tower and bailey

Archaeological and reconstruction work began after 1870, where a major concern was the stability of the rock base on which the castle stands. It has since been excellently restored. At present, the hrad is open to the public, and contains an informative museum. It is a designated National Cultural Monument.

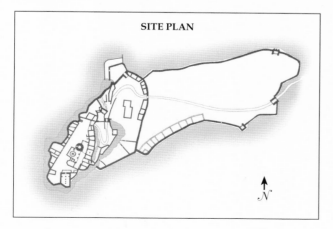

SITE PLAN

Facing page:
Spišský Hrad was a textbook castle with all the elements of castle design. It occupies the summit of a large dolomite hill and there have been concerns in the past about the stability of the site.

View from the upper castle, looking down towards the lower bailey and the outer castle yard.

A cannon from the weapons display in the castle museum.

SLOVENIA

Bled

Ljubljana

Bled Castle

Bled Castle is located at the edge of a steep cliff, with a sharp drop from its ramparts into Lake Bled below. It is the oldest castle in Slovenia — the first title deed to the estate of Bled dates to 1011, when it was given to the Bishops of Brixen by Emperor Henry II. The clergy built a strong castle on this remote site, and ruled the area with an iron hand, which led to periods of serious unrest among the populace, and an armed revolt in 1515. The Archdiocese eventually sold the castle around 1860. It was occupied by the Germans in World War II.

The oldest part of the castle is the Romanesque Tower. A 16th-century chapel has fine Gothic exterior pillars and Baroque paintings. The distinctive red-tiled roofs of the castle are easily visible from the lake waters. A steep, paved path leads up to a drawbridge at the entrance. The castle yard is on several levels, the highest of which afford some magnificent views of the Julian Alps. The castle was rebuilt many times through its 1000-year history.

ADDRESS	Cesta svobode 11, 4260 Bled, Slovenia
CONSTRUCTION HISTORY	**11th century** First structures; round tower
	1622 Destroyed in fire
	1690 Damaged in earthquake
	1951–61 renovation of interiors
COMMISSIONED BY	Bishops of Brixen
MATERIALS	Stone, tile
STYLE	Rock castle; Gothic, Romanesque

The castle is now the property of the Republic of Slovenia. Conveniently located just 33 miles (54 km) north-west of Ljubljana, it attracts scores of visitors, and is a venue for conferences, exhibitions and weddings. It also maintains a museum displaying the different phases of the castle's history. Also of interest are the printing works, which have a copy of Gutenberg's printing press, and an herbal gallery.

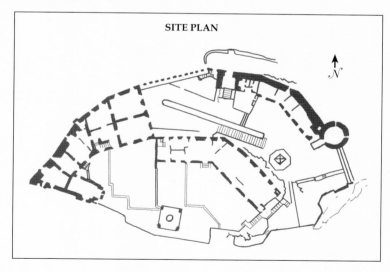

SITE PLAN

A perimeter tower crowned with red tiles. Covered passages connected different parts of the castle.

Castle forecourt.

Facing page:
The spectacularly located Bled Castle has stunning views of the Julian Alps and the lake below. The Bishops of Brixen owned the castle for nearly eight centuries.

SPAIN

• Madrid

• Alhambra

Alhambra Castle

By the 10th century, a large part of the Iberian Peninsula was ruled by the Moors, who brought Islamic styles of military and domestic architecture to Spain. The majestic citadel of Alhambra, in the mountainous kingdom of Granada, combines within its walls the *alcazaba* or a typical Muslim garrison fortress, as well as the *alcázar* or the royal palace. It was built by the Nasrid sultans who ruled Granada till 1492, when it was retaken by the Catholic armies after an eight-month siege. In the 16th century, Charles V built an imposing Renaissance palace within the fort walls. To the east of the Alhambra complex are the magnificent gardens of the Generalife, dating to the 13th century.

An elongated enclosure follows the contours of the ridge, and is bounded by an adobe wall with 13 square mural towers. The main entranceway or the Justice Gate was a vaulted passageway with three right-angled turns. At the narrow eastern end of the citadel is the fortified *alcazaba*, with the Torre de la Vela and the Quebrada towers. It is protected by a strong wall and dry ditches. Towards its west is the *alcázar*, which is a complex of royal and administrative chambers set around rectangular courts, the most spectacular being the Court of the Lions, the Court of the Myrtles and the Hall of the Ambassadors. Succeeding rulers added new wings, and over the years the Alhambra developed into a paradisiacal arrangement of fountains, scented gardens, and interlinked palaces exquisitely decorated in the mudéjar style. Elaborate stucco and tile work, brilliantly colored enameling, and detailed stone and wood carving coexist in a stunning amalgam of geometric and floral motifs, and calligraphic inscriptions. Also of note is the 'stalactite vaulting', which is a term used for intricate honeycomb patterning inside a domed ceiling.

ADDRESS	Alhambra, Calle Real del Alhambra, 18009 Granada
CONSTRUCTION HISTORY	**Ninth century** First fortification
	1236–73 Walled enclosure with mural towers, *alcazaba*
	1334–1408 *Alcázar* or palace complex built; wall of *alcazaba* extended
	15th century Some structures demolished, interiors damaged and whitewashed
	1527–80s Palace of Charles V of Spain
COMMISSIONED BY	Nasrid rulers of Granada
MATERIALS	Brick and stone
STYLE	Rock castle; Moorish

After centuries of neglect, the Alhambra was rediscovered in the 19th century by European travelers, after which it has been gradually restored.

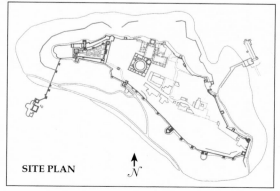

Facing page:
Alhambra or the 'Red One', named for the red stone used in its construction, was the impregnable stronghold of the Nasrid sultans, located high in the mountains of Granada. It was famous for its exquisite interiors and landscaped gardens.

SITE PLAN

The Court of the Myrtles is reflected in its courtyard pool.

The intricate carving of the walls and pillars are the finest examples of Spanish mudéjar decoration.

Fuensaldaña

Madrid

SPAIN

Fuensaldaña Castle

The redistribution of lands following the Reconquista created a newly ennobled class of Spanish society that entered upon a spate of castle building in a conscious effort to display their wealth and gain acceptance among the old aristocracy. Around the 1450s, the Duero valley in Castile saw the emergence of a distinctive 'Valladolid' castle style that emulated the royal castles of Enrique VI at Medina del Campo and Torre Nuevo in Segovia. Each castle was on a square plan, with the height of the wall equal to half the length of its side. The characteristic Spanish *Torre del Homenaje* or Homage Tower was located on one side, its height being twice that of the wall. The small castle at Fuensaldaña, located 4 miles from Valladolid, also followed this proportion. It was built around 1453 by Alonso Pérez de Vivero, Treasurer to King Juan II, with probable assistance from a Muslim master mason. However, Alonso was killed soon afterwards by a political rival at the court, and his castle remained uninhabited.

The building's red and ochre tints, as well as compact formation, bring to mind a Roman desert fortress. The square castle wall has round angle towers and corbeled bartizans located midway on three sides. The rectangular four-story *Torre del Homenaje* sits on the third side. It also has slender corner towers and bartizans, and in times of trouble, the Tower could be easily isolated from the rest of the castle. It functioned as the main residence, and was reached via a bridge from a free-standing stairway in the castle bailey. Other domestic quarters that were placed around the bailey walls are now in ruins. The machicolations and merlons on the battlements are in the mudéjar style.

The Torre del Homenaje and castle battlements.

ADDRESS	Castillo de Fuensaldaña, Fuensaldaña 47194, Spain
CONSTRUCTION PERIOD	Mid-15th century
COMMISSIONED BY	Alonso Pérez de Vivero
MATERIALS	Stone
STYLE	Tower keep and bailey; Valladolid

Fuensaldaña has been restored and is in use by several government departments. It is open to the public by appointment.

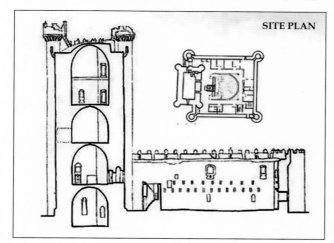

SITE PLAN

Facing page:
The imposing Torre del Homenaje *or Homage Tower was typical of the Valladolid style of castle construction. It was exactly double the height of the curtain wall.*

The main gateway into the castle.

Segovia

Madrid

SPAIN

Alcázar at Segovia

Segovia was one of the early victories of the Reconquista, and the *alcázar*—a Moorish term for a palace—was first built by Alfonso VI in the 11th century. It was planned on the site of an earlier Moorish fort, atop a rocky crag at the confluence of the Eresma and Calmores rivers. Constructed in a Romanesque-Gothic style, it was the principal residence of the Castilian monarchs until the court moved to Madrid in the late 16th century. It remained in use as a state prison for the next two centuries, after which the Royal Artillery School was founded here in 1762. Large parts of the castle were damaged in a devastating fire in 1862. Restoration work began soon afterwards, and the *Alcázar* was handed over to the Ministry of War in 1896.

The most imposing structure in this *gran buque*, or boat-shaped, castle is the tall *Torre del Homenaje* or Homage Tower of Juan II. Its austere exterior is enlivened with 12 slender bartizans and a machicolated parapet. Towards the prow of the castle lies the second, square donjon, with slim flanking towers. Its conical roofs, reminiscent of Central European castles, were the handiwork of Felipe II in the 16th century. The royal apartments are wedged around the courtyards, each chamber lavishly decorated and painted in a mix of Gothic and mudéjar style, the latter a mix of Islamic and Christian elements very typical of Spain. Many of the velvet and silk furnishings are original, as are the paintings and furniture. The Kings Room contains a frieze with 52 seated sculptures, originally thought to be in gold, of the monarchs of Asturias, Castile and Leon.

ADDRESS	Plaza de la Reina Victoria Eugenia, S/N, 40003 Segovia, Spain
CONSTRUCTION HISTORY	**11th century** Boat-shaped citadel
	1258 Rebuilt
	Early 15th century New Tower
	16th century Conical slate roofs
	1587 Gardens by Francisco de Morar
COMMISSIONED BY	Alfonso VI of Castile
MATERIALS	Stone, plaster and timber
STYLE	Rock castle with tower and bailey; *gran buque*

The castle still functions as a School of Artillery and contains the Military Archives. In 1951, the Patronato del Alcázar was created to co-ordinate its various functions and the ongoing restoration, as well as manage the Museum of the Alcázar of Segovia.

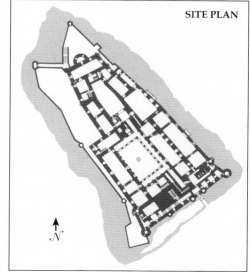

SITE PLAN

N

Facing page:
Slender towers with pointed caps give Segovia a fairytale appearance. However, the gun loops in the tower are evidence of its military use.

The castle keep has meticulous mudéjar work, as seen in its detailed corbelling and wall decoration

A stained glass window in the Alcázar with the Arms of Castile and Leon shown below the knight.

Peñafiel

Madrid

SPAIN

Castillo de Peñafiel

According to legend, when King Sancho of Castile wrested Valladolid from the Moors in the 11th century, he drove his sword into the rock at the highest point on a nearby crag and declared it to be the "*Peñafiel* (faithful rock) of Castile!" The Christian castle that came up on this site was built over an earlier Moorish fort, and controled for a time by a lieutenant of the famous El Cid. The present castle owes much to the efforts of Don Pedro de Giron, Master of the Order of Calatrava, who added many modifications in the 15th century. Don Juan Manuel, the literary minded nephew of King Alfonso the Wise, lived at Peñafiel in the early14th century where he wrote his famous *El Conde Lucanor*, one of the earliest significant works of prose in Castilian Spanish.

Peñafiel is one of the best *gran buque* (boat-shaped) castles in Spain. Elongated in shape, its high inner curtain wall is 690 ft (210 m) in length, but measures only 74 ft (22 m) at the widest point. There is a single cylindrical tower at the pointed bow and another at the center of the short stern wall. Six round towers and 21 corbeled turrets are spaced at intervals along the longer sides. A continuous wall walk and machicolated battlements add to its defenses, and a lower outer wall encircles the hilltop.

The massive 15th century *Torre del Homenaje* is placed at the center of the citadel, dividing it into the north and south baileys. A gate in the outer wall leads into the inner bailey by means of an angled pathway that turns once again sharply to enter the keep.

ADDRESS	Castillo de Peñafiel, Peñafiel 47300 - Spain
CONSTRUCTION PERIOD	11th–15th century
	10th century Moorish fort
	11–14th century Wall towers; inner and outer curtain
	15th century *Gran buque* completed, main tower and entrances.
COMMISSIONED BY	Kings of Castile
MATERIALS	Local stone
STYLE	Keep and bailey

At present, the Museo Provincial del Vino (Wine Museum) is located in the castle. The castle battlements provide a splendid view of the Duero valley. The castle is open to the public.

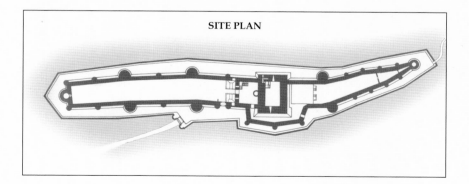

SITE PLAN

The castle yard narrows at one end to meet at a point, like the prow of a ship.

The high central keep stands like a wheelhouse at the center of the castle.

Facing page:
Peñafiel was one of the early victories of the Reconquista. Its walls blend with the rock face on which they stand.

Castillo de la Mota

Madrid

SPAIN

Castillo de la Mota

Castillo de la Mota is located on a *mota* or a hill at Medina Del Campo in Valladolid, an area of Spain famous for its Gothic-mudéjar castles. This imposing brick fortification continues the regional tradition, and the earliest castle here dates to the 12th century. The castle was rebuilt many times by the Castilian kings, and what is seen today is the impressive structure erected in the 1460s under the direction of two architects, Fernando Carreño and Alonso Nieta. For much of its history, the Castillo remained in the hands of the Castilian monarchy, though there were frequent clashes with the rival rulers of Aragon. After the historic marriage alliance of Isabel and Ferdinand in 1469, the united Arms of Aragon and Castile were engraved upon the main entranceway. In the 16th century, it was a state prison, housing the likes of Hernando Pizzaro, Rodrigo Calderon and Cesare Borgia. The last engineered a legendary escape by letting himself down by a rope from the tower window on to a waiting horse.

The inner bailey has a massive *Torre del Homenaje* and rectangular corner towers, while the outer bailey has lower round angle towers and two gateway towers. The *Torre del Homenaje* sports the twin bartizan pattern that can also be seen in the *alcázar* at Segovia. A deep moat separated the two baileys. Gun loops are visible along the length of the outer curtain, which also has a covered, vaulted *chemin de ronde*. Built entirely of brick, except for some stone detailing, Castillo de la Mota is another example of Spanish mudéjar style, which is a pleasing mix of Christian Gothic and Moorish elements.

ADDRESS	Avenida del Castillo 47400 Medina del Campo, Valladolid, Spain
CONSTRUCTION HISTORY	**12th century** Moorish fort
	13–15th century Inner keep with Homage Tower and four rectangular towers; outer curtain wall with round flanking towers, two gate towers, mid-point semi-circular towers, gun loops, *chemin de ronde*
	1940s Restoration work began
COMMISSIONED BY	Kings of Castile
ARCHITECTS	Fernando Carreño and Alonso Nieta (15th century)
MATERIALS	Brick, tile
STYLE	Concentric castle with tower keep; Gothic-mudéjar

Restoration efforts began under the Franco administration. At present, the castillo is owned and managed by the Junta de Castile y Leon, and is a major conference venue as well as a popular tourist attraction.

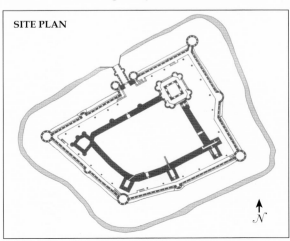
SITE PLAN
N

Facing page:
Castillo de la Mota has a special place in Castilian history. The tall Torre del Homenage (Homage Tower) has twin corbelled bartizans, seen in many Spanish castles.

The arms of Castile and Aragon are engraved over the main entranceway.

An inner courtyard.

Castillo de Coca

In 1453, the wealthy and influential Bishop of Seville, Don Alonso de Fonseca, received permission from King Juan II to raise a fortified castle on his lands in Segovia. Accordingly, work began on the construction of a splendid Gothic-mudéjar edifice at Coca, under the direction of master mason Ali. Built on a grand scale, it is one of the most striking examples of Christian and Moorish military architecture in Spain. The interiors were lavishly decorated as Bishop Alonso lived luxuriously and entertained on a grand scale. By the 16th century, Coca had passed to the Dukes of Alba. Though equipped for artillery, the castillo was never seriously besieged, except once rather ineffectively by the lovelorn swain of a Fonseca lady around 1504. It remained largely unchallenged until taken by Napoleon's armies in 1808.

Located in the plains, the castle was protected by a wide and deep moat. A concentric fortress is formed by an outer and inner wall encircling a square bailey. Octagonal towers flank three corners, while the fourth has the larger keep or the *Torre del Homenaje*. A profusion of bartizans sprout from the towers, and also at midpoints along the inner curtain wall. There are cross-shaped gun loops and casemates at the corner towers for artillery warfare. Built mostly of brick, the Castillo displays a wealth of Moorish decorative detail in the exterior and the interior. Fussy crenellations line the battlements, and intricate stucco work can be seen in the chambers, particularly the Fish Room and the Hall of Jugs. The Arms Hall has a fine Gothic vaulted ceiling and multi-colored geometric mosaic on the walls.

ADDRESS	Camino Antigua Cauca Romana, 40480 Coca, Segovia, Spain
CONSTRUCTION HISTORY	**1473** Construction of fortified castle-palace; moat, inner and outer walls; towers and keep
	1504 Defenses extended
	1950s Restoration work
COMMISSIONED BY	Alfonso Fonseca, Archbishop of Seville
MATERIALS	Limestone and brick
STYLE	Gothic, mudéjar

The Castillo de Coca was leased to the Ministry of Agriculture in 1951. Restored in phases during the 1950s, it now houses the Forestry Training Institute. It is open to the public.

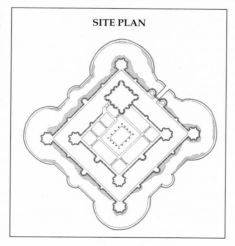

SITE PLAN

Elegant galleries around an interior courtyard.

The intricate merlons on the battlements are typical of Spanish mudéjar craftsmanship.

Facing page:
Originally circled by a deep moat, the Castillo de Coca was a strongly fortified bishopric palace.

SWEDEN

Stockholm

Kalmar

Kalmar Castle

This legendary castle, nicknamed 'The Key to Sweden' is located on the southeastern coast of the country, in the province of Smaland. Around 800 years ago, a fortified tower was built at this vantage site as protection against the Vikings and other sea-faring raiders. King Magnus Ladulås (r. 1275–90) expanded the harbor, and built a castle bailey around the tower. Kalmar was the venue for the signing of the Union of Kalmar pact on 20 July, 1397, one of the most significant and contentious events in Nordic history, which joined Sweden, Norway and Denmark under a common ruler. During the Swedish rebellion against Denmark, it was valiantly defended by Anna Eriksdotter, who took over the command of the castle in 1520. In the 16th century, it was transformed into a Renaissance citadel by the Vasa kings. The last ruler to reside in the castle was Charles XI (r. 1673–92). It gradually fell into disrepair until restored between 1856–1941.

Round flanking towers made their first appearance in Sweden at Kalmar in the 13th century. The original curtain wall is an irregular circle with two square gate towers. Outer ramparts and squat, round artillery bastions were added in the 16th century. Renaissance details are seen in the well-appointed interiors of the Green Hall and the Banqueting Hall, as well as in the elegant roofs and spires of the towers.

ADDRESS	Kungsgatan 1 392 33 Kalmar, Sweden
CONSTRUCTION HISTORY	**12th century** Defensive tower
	13th century Curtain wall with flanking round towers, domestic ranges and square gate towers; protected harbor developed
	15th–16th century Rebuilding and renovation; artillery bastions
	17th century Damaged by war and fire
	1856 Interiors restored by Fredrik Scholander
	1880s Restoration continued by Carl Möller
	1919–41 Earthworks, moat, and drawbridge repaired by Martin Olssen
COMMISSIONED BY	Kings of Sweden
ARCHITECTS	Jacob Richter, Johan Baptista, Dominicus Pahr (16th century)
MATERIALS	Stone and timber
STYLE	Harbor castle; Keep and bailey

Kalmar is one of Sweden's best preserved historic monuments, and is managed by the Swedish National Property Board. In 1997, it celebrated the 100th anniversary of the Kalmar Pact. The county museum is also housed here, and the castle is also a popular venue for banquets and weddings.

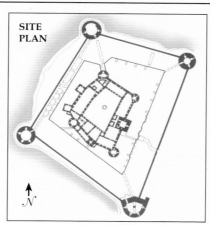

SITE PLAN

N

Facing page:
A significant castle in Sweden's history, Kalmar presents a striking vista of sturdy red walls and elegant tower caps and spires.

The castle church that dates to the late 16th century.

Coat of Arms at Kalmar Castle.

SWEDEN

Stockholm

Visby

Visby and Visborg

The fortified town of Visby on the island of Gotland, in the Baltic Sea, was a prosperous commercial center from the 10th to the 14th century, and a prominent member of the influential League of Hanseatic towns. Its sturdy ring wall or *ringmuren*, enclosed over 200 warehouses and burghers dwellings, as well as several churches. In 1361, King Vlademer IV of Denmark landed his army in Gotland, and the townspeople fought a bloody and ultimately losing battle against the invaders. Gotland remained under Danish rule for 300 years, and by the 15th century, Visby had become a haven for all manner of pirates and sea brigands. In 1411, the dispossessed monarch, Eric of Pomerania, made Visby his home, and erected Visborg castle. Gotland was reconquered by Sweden in 1665.

The town walls represent the earliest use of flanking towers in Scandinavia. All the towers are open-backed, with wooden platforms being erected for defense. They are rectangular structures from the base to the level of the wall, then transform into semi-octagonal rounds. This was probably to clear a line of vision for bowmen, as well as provide a solid base to deter sappers. Between each tower is a smaller tower, corbeled out of the wall. Visborg castle is at the southwest corner, with the wall running through it. It is exceptionally plain, consisting of a square enclosure with corner towers.

The town walls at Visby with open-backed flanking towers.

ADDRESS	Visby, Gotland 62155, Sweden
CONSTRUCTION HISTORY	**12–13th century** Town ringmuren, 2 ½ miles (4km) in extent, with 30ft (9m) high rectangular towers.
	1225 Visby cathedral consecrated
	1411 Visborg castle
	1679 castle partly demolished
COMMISSIONED BY	Burghers of Visby (town wall); Eric of Pomerania (Visborg Castle)
MATERIALS	Stone
STYLE	Fortified town

The *ringmuren* is largely intact, and Visby is one of the best preserved fortifications in Sweden. It is a popular attraction, especially in the summer months. In July, Visby hosts the annual gathering of Swedish politicians called Almedalen Week, and in August there is a medieval festival with markets, fairs, music, and food of a bygone age.

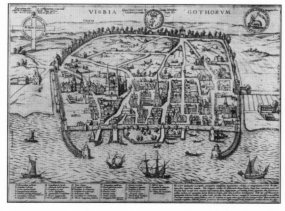

Facing page: A section of the ringmuren or the town wall at Visby, which has survived from the early Middle Ages.
Above: A 16th-century engraving of the town of Visby.

A painting depicting Visby harbor as it may have looked in its heydey, as a prosperous trading post in the Baltic.

SWITZERLAND

Bern

Aigle

Château d'Aigle

Nestled at the foot of the Bernese Alps amid verdant, lush vineyards, Château d'Aigle or Eagle Castle is a picture of romantic perfection. It falls in the Canton of Vaud, 29 miles southeast of Lausanne, but in the 12th century it was the French speaking domain of the Savoyard dukes. They enfranchised the town of Aigle, which grew to be an important commercial center. In the 12th century, the Saillon family built a castle around a previously existing square donjon on behalf of the Dukes of Savoy. In 1475, the castle was captured and burnt by the Bernese. Rebuilt again, it became the residence of the Bernese provincial governors till 1798. After the French Revolution, the château was purchased by the town of Aigle in 1804, and became the county prison till 1832. Besides its exceptional wine, Aigle is also known for being the first French speaking area to turn officially Protestant, through the efforts of the 16th century reformist preacher Guillamme Farel.

The château follows a roughly rectangular plan. Narrow round towers sit at three corners, while the earlier square donjon with supporting turrets is at the fourth corner. Savoyard influence is visible in the conical roofs. A covered walk runs along the entire perimeter of the curtain wall, and a gatehouse projects over the main entranceway.

ADDRESS	Château d'Aigle CH-1860 Aigle Switzerland
CONSTRUCTION HISTORY	**11th century** square tower or donjon
	12th–15th century castle wall, round towers and domestic ranges
	1475 Partially burnt and damaged
	1480s Rebuilt and extended
	1972 Restoration underway
COMMISSIONED BY	Dukes of Savoy
MATERIALS	Stone
STYLE	Donjon, bailey; Savoyard

Several phases of restoration began in 1972, and the work still continues. In 1971, the Brotherhood of Guillon established a Museum of Vine, Wine and Label at the castle, to preserve and showcase the centuries-old tradition of winemaking in the Leman region. Every aspect of the vintner's art is exhibited in 17 rooms of the castle, elaborating on topics such as biodiversity and ecology of the region, development of taste, well-known vineyards and vintages, and festivals of wine. There is also a collection of wine bottle labels from 52 countries.

The round angle towers with the typical Savoyard conical roofs.

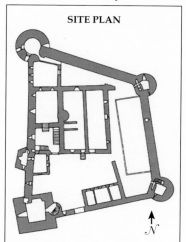

SITE PLAN

N

Facing page:
A birds-eye view of the Château d' Aigle, surrounded by acres of vineyards.

A man dressed as a medieval troubadour stands at a doorway in the castle.

SWITZERLAND

Bern

Chillon

Château de Chillon

Located on island on the eastern edge of Lac Leman or Lake Geneva, the venerable Château de Chillon guarded the route from Italy into Switzerland from early medieval times. The eclectic collection of buildings and courtyards within its grey stone walls is testimony to several centuries of occupation and activity. Its earliest reference dates to the 10th century, when it belonged to the Bishops of Sion. In the 12th century, Chillon passed to the Dukes of Savoy. In 1536, it was captured by the Bernese Swiss who used it as an armaments store for their flotilla in the lake. Lord Byron's well-known poem, *The Prisoner of Chillon,* refers to François Bonnivard, a Swiss hero who had been imprisoned at the château for four years before being released by the Bernese. The Canton of Vaud received the castle in 1798.

The rectangular tower in the center of the bailey is probably the oldest structure in the castle. Peter II, Duke of Savoy, employed Peter Mainier to supervise the building of the outer wall, towers, and many other structures in the 13th century. His brother Philippe of Savoy entrusted the task to the master engineer Jacques de Saint-Georges d'Espéranche , who later built formidable castles for Edward I of England. The Savoyard elements can be seen in the full-centered arches at the walls, and the window arches. The first courtyard contained military offices; the second had the prefect's chambers, magazines and dungeons. The Count's residence and chapel abutted the third courtyard. In 1836, the castle was mainly an ammunition and artillery store, and the courtyard entrances were widened to allow the passage of cannons.

ADDRESS	xxxxxxxxxxx
CONSTRUCTION HISTORY	**10th century** rectangular tower
	13th century outer wall, three D-shaped towers, gatehouse, inner buildings around the lakeside wall; machicolations on battlements and towers
	14th–15th century height added to walls and towers; gate rebuilt
COMMISSIONED BY	Peter II of Savoy
ARCHITECTS	Peter Mainier; Jacques de St George
MATERIALS	Grey sandstone
STYLE	Island castle; Savoyard

Chillon's picturesque location has attracted visitors since the mid-18th century and it continues to be one of the most popular attractions in Switzerland. Since 2002, it has been managed by the Foundation of the Castle of Chillon, that has also taken on the task of restoration and conservation.

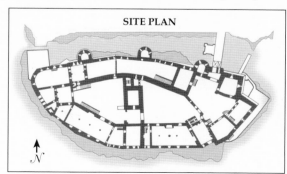

SITE PLAN

Facing page:
The Château de Chillon, surrounded by the waters of the Lac Leman, is a superb example of Savoyard architecture.

The Great Hall of the Count has slender black marble pillars, checkered wall decoration, and a coffered ceiling dating from the 15th century. Its windows have an elegant four-leafed clover design.

Stairs leading down to the castle basement, which was also used as a prison.

• Qalaat Saladin

SYRIA

• Damascus

Qalaat Saladin

This remarkable rock citadel is located high in the mountains of Syria in the region of Latakia, at the junction of two streams. There was a Byzantine fort at this site, which fell to the Crusader knights at the beginning of the 12th century. Robert of Saone was entrusted the castle by Robert of Antioch around 1119, and it came to be called Saone Castle. Though inaccessible and well-defended, the castle was taken by the indomitable Saladin in 1188, and thus acquired its present name of Qalaat Saladin. Some of the gigantic stone catapults used by Saladin's siege engines can still be seen in the castle grounds. It was controlled by several noble families until begin taken over by Sultan Qalaun in 1287.

The castle has an elongated shape, and is demarcated into a lower, middle and upper bailey. The most remarkable feature is the hand-hewn ditch cut into the rock face, along the side where the castle is backed up against the mountain. To create this 450 ft (140 m) long, 60 ft (18 m) deep ditch, the Crusaders displaced nearly 170,000 tons of solid rock. This was used to rebuild the castle. A slender pillar of rock was left standing in the ditch to serve as the sole support of the drawbridge across the gap.

The crusaders built square defensive towers along the south. These did not project much out of the curtain wall, a fact that may have limited their defensive capacity. A long rectangular tower flanked the main entrance passage, and water was stored in two subterranean cisterns. The main keep and residential buildings were at the highest point in the upper ward, backed by the rock ditch and mountain.

ADDRESS	xxxxx
CONSTRUCTION HISTORY	**10th century** Byzantine fortress
	12th– 13th century Walls expanded; towers; ditch; donjon
	14th–16th century Mosque, palace, baths
COMMISSIONED BY	Byzantine emperors; Crusader knights
MATERIALS	Limestone
STYLE	Rock castle

Deserted over the centuries, the castle eventually became a ruin, overgrown with vegetation. At present, it is open to the public, and receives many visitors despite its remote location and difficult terrain.

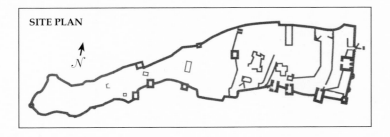

SITE PLAN

The dizzying view from the citadel.

The needle of rock left standing in the deep, man-made ditch to serve as a support for the drawbidge.

Facing page:
Known as Saone Castle by the crusaders, this is one of the best-preserved of the castles built by the Christian knights.

SYRIA
• Krak des Chevaliers

• Damascus

Krak des Chevaliers

Located on a prominent rocky spur 90 miles (145km) from Damascus, Krak des Chevaliers is the most well preserved of medieval Crusader fortresses. Originally a small Kurdish fort, it was granted to the Knights Hospitaller by the Count of Tripoli in 1142. The Knights constructed an impregnable concentric castle to defend the Crusader Christian kingdoms, and the pilgrimage routes in the Holy Land. The castle dominated the valley between Homs and Tripoli, and thus controlled the access to the sea.

At the peak of its power, the Krak des Chevaliers housed nearly 2000 men and their horses. In 1163, it successfully withstood a siege by Nur-ud-din Zengi, and fended off an attack by Saladin in 1188. It was finally conquered in 1271 by the Mameluks, and legend has it that this was done was by means of a forged letter from the Crusader commander in Tripoli, asking the defenders to surrender.

The outer curtain wall was punctuated at intervals by cylindrical guard towers. A moat separated it from the high inner ramparts that were up to 100 ft (30m) thick and ringed by a smooth slope called 'glacis', rendering them impossible to climb. The colossal outer gate led into a vaulted corridor with hairpin bends that rose steeply upwards. A graceful colonnade in the inner keep opened into a vaulted Gothic hall containing an oven and a well. A beautiful Romanesque chapel (later converted to a mosque) stood next to the courtyard. Storage rooms were carved into the rock below the castle.

ADDRESS	Homs Governate, Syria
CONSTRUCTION HISTORY	**11th century** rectangular Arab fortress 'Hisn al Akrad' or Castle of the Kurds
	1142 Castle enclosure with square towers
	1170 Earthquake causes some damage; repairs undertaken; new chapel
	1202 Another earthquake; walls strengthened
	1271 Large square tower and a round corner tower rebuilt
BUILT BY	The Hospitaller Order of St. John of Jerusalem
MATERIALS	Limestone
STYLE	Rock castle; Romanesque, Gothic

T E Lawrence described the Krak des Chevaliers as 'the best preserved and most wholly admirable castle in the world.' It one of the main tourist attractions in Syria.

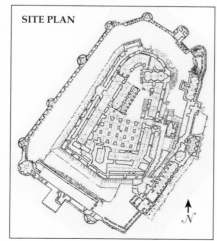

SITE PLAN

Facing page:
Kraks des Chevaliers remained unvanquished in battle throughout its history.

The raised inner keep presented a 360 degree view of the countryside.

The Gothic windows of the castle chapel, which was converted to a mosque.

SYRIA

Margat

Damascus

Margat Castle

Also known as Qalaat Marghab, this castle was one of the prominent strongholds of the Knights Hospitaller, a crusading military order active in the Holy Lands during medieval times. Located on a hill at the edge of the Syrian coast near Baniyas, it was originally an Arab fortress before being conquered by the Byzantines, and then by the Principality of Antioch in the 1120s. Around 1186, it was sold to the Knights Hospitaller who expanded it into their headquarters in Syria. It withstood an onslaught by Saladin in 1188, and by the 13th century, Margat was firmly in control of the pilgrim routes in the region. Bishops and kings broke journey here, and it was second only to Krak des Chevalier in size and strength. However, it was taken in 1285 after a month long siege by the Mamluk sultan Qalaun, whose sappers successfully mined the south tower.

Unlike the Krak, Margat is not a perfect concentric castle. It has a triangular shape that follows the slope of the ridge, and its 14 towers gave an enormous impression of impregnability. A dry ditch protected the inner bailey. The castle chapel was a Gothic masterpiece, and it has survived, along with some barrel vaulted chambers. Time and neglect have taken their toll on the castle, and much of it is in a ruined state.

ADDRESS	Governate of Tartous, Syria
CONSTRUCTION HISTORY	**10th century** Arab fort
	12th century expanded
	12th–13th century Keep, walls and towers
COMMISSIONED BY	The Hospitaller Order of St. John of Jerusalem
MATERIALS	Basalt
STYLE	Rock castle

The castle remained occupied until Ottoman times, when it was a remote military outpost of the empire. At present, it is open to the public.

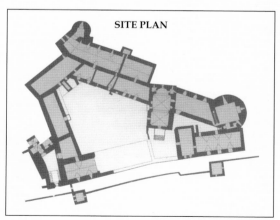

SITE PLAN

One of the castle's large, circular towers.

A view ot the castle grounds.

Facing page:
The formidable Margat Castle was a stronghold of the Knights Hospitaller, known for their skills in building impregnable fortifications.

Roumelihisari

Ankara   **TURKEY**

Roumelihisari

The massive fortress of Roumelihisari is located on a steep hill in the Sariyer district of Istanbul. It stands on the European side of the Bosphorus strait, looking across the water at the Anadoulihisari, its counterpart on the Asiatic shore. The most striking feature of this castle is the fearsome Black Tower at the waterfront, which was probably built by the Byzantine emperor Alexios Comnenus around 1100. In 1452, the Turkish sultan Mehmed II rebuilt Roumelihisari, with the intention of creating a strong base for his assault on Constantinople, planned for the following spring of 1453. Cannons installed on top of the Black Tower controlled shipping on the straits, and the castle came to be known as 'Boghaz Kenen', or 'Cutter of the Throat'. After the fall of Constantinople, it was a customs point, and was eventually abandoned by the 19th century.

The crenellated walls of the fort follow the gradient of the slope down towards the water. The Black Tower derived its name from the utter darkness that prevailed in its interior chambers, due to the conspicuous lack of window apertures in the walls that have a thickness of 24 ft (7 m). It was originally a prison, and an unusual feature here is the presence of an oubliette, or a deep chamber with a door set high in the wall, and no windows. Prisoners were literally pushed into oblivion from above. The Turks added two stories, and the tower, renamed the Halil Pasha Tower, continued as a dreaded prison. Two other towers, namely the Zaganos Pasha, and the Sarica Pasha, and a strong curtain wall with 13 watch towers, were also constructed in a record time of just over four months, under the personal supervision of the Sultan.

The walls of the castle reach down to the edge of the Bosphorus.

ADDRESS	xxxxx
CONSTRUCTION HISTORY	1100 Black Tower;
	1450 Curtain wall, watchtowers, main towers; cannon
	1953 Restoration work begins
COMMISSIONED BY	Sultan Mehmed II
MATERIALS	Stone
STYLE	Tower and curtain wall; Byzantine; Ottoman

At present, the castle is a museum and is open to the public. It also hosts open air concerts and theatrical productions.

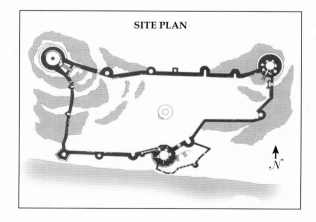
SITE PLAN

Facing page:
The three main towers of the fortress, namely Halil Pasha, Zaganos Pasha and Sarica Pasha, were named after Sultan Mehmet II's viziers, who supervized their construction. Roumelihisari was a staging point for the Turkish conquest of Constantinople in 1453.

Halil Pasha Tower, known earlier as the Black Tower.

TURKEY

Ankara

Bodrun

Bodrun St Peter

Bodrum Kalesi or the Castle of St Peter encompasses a tiny island opposite Kos, in southwest Turkey. It is a remarkable piece of military engineering built in the 15th century by the Knights Hospitaller, a medieval military order of knights based in Rhodes. Faced with the growing threat of Seljuk Turkey in this part of the Mediterranean, Grandmaster Philibert de Naillac ordered the construction of Bodrum Castle on the site of an earlier fort. Unfortunately, the stone for building was obtained by dismantling the ancient Mausoleum of Halicarnassus, which was also on the island. Construction continued till 1450, and the castle successfully repelled Turkish attacks between 1453 and 1480.

In 1522, Rhodes castle yielded to the Turks, and the terms of surrender including the handing over of the castles at Bodrun and Kos. Thereafter it became a Turkish garrison fort and prison. It was abandoned in 1921, after a brief Italian occupation.

As in Rhodes, different sections of the wall were entrusted to the national sub-groups among the Knights, who each maintained their own troops, and were responsible for the safety of their portion of the castle. The French Tower is the tallest, followed by the English Tower, also called the Lion Tower. Hundreds of painted coat of arms and carved escutcheon panels line the walls of the castle.

The Gothic chapel was converted to a mosque after 1522. In the mid-19th century, excavations unearthed and removed numerous carved reliefs from the castle walls that originally belonged to the ancient Greek tomb.

ADDRESS	48400 Bodrum, Turkey
CONSTRUCTION HISTORY	**1406** Chapel
	1413 English Tower completed
	1494 Walls thickened
	1520 Chapel rebuilt in Gothic style
	1501–22 Artillery outworks
COMMISSIONED BY	The Knights Hospitaller
MATERIALS	Stone
STYLE	Sea castle; Byzantine

At present, the castle is open to the public, and houses the Bodrum Museum of Underwater Archeology which displays a fascinating collection of objects retrieved from shipwrecks in the Aegean Sea. There are also collections of ancient glass objects, coinage, and an extensive garden within the castle walls.

A stained-glass window in the English Tower with the arms of the Knights Hospitaller.

Facing page:
A section of the walls and towers of Bodrum Castle. As in other Crusader castles, it was built with material salvaged from ancient sites, in this case from the Tomb of Halicarnassus.

The battlements and towers of the castle.

USA

Boldt

Washington DC

Boldt Castle

Boldt Castle is located on Heart Island which is among the Thousand Island group in the St Lawrence River, near the northern border of New York state. It was the inspired creation of millionaire George C Boldt, proprietor of the Waldorf-Astoria Hotel in New York. Around the turn of the century, the Boldt family spent several memorable summers in this picturesque location. In 1900, George Boldt hired the firm of GW&WD Hewitt to construct a modern-day castle on Heart Island. Work began immediately on a vast structure of masonry, incorporating every luxury and convenience of the time. Unfortunately, the project was abandoned because of the sudden demise of Louise Boldt in 1904. The heartbroken husband never returned to the site, which remained untouched till 1977, when the Thousand Island Authority purchased the estate for one dollar, on the condition that they would restore and preserve the building for future generations.

The original plan included a six-story castle in the Rhineland style, with a drawbridge, tunnels, 120 rooms, an Italianate garden, an indoor pool, a dovecote and a power house. An adjacent island, with an existing summer home, was to contain tennis courts, a golf course, riding stables and a polo lawn. An exposed masonry surfacing was used to add a touch of European authenticity. Since 1977 an expensive restoration programme has rebuilt the castle to the point that it was abandoned in 1904. New features have also been added such as a stained-glass dome, a marble floor, and a grand wooden staircase.

The Alster Tower was to be the playhouse, with a bowling alley, billiards room, dance floor and library.

ADDRESS	Heart Island, Alexandria Bay, New York 13607, USA
CONSTRUCTION HISTORY	**1900** Construction begins
	1904 construction halted
	1977 to date Restoration and new construction/ refurbishing
COMMISSIONED BY	George C Boldt
MATERIALS	Stone, timber, tile
STYLE	Island castle; 20th century American

Since 1977, an expensive restoration programme has rebuilt the castle to the point that it was abandoned in 1904. New features have also been added, such as a stained-glass dome, a marble floor, and a grand wooden staircase.

Heart Island is open to the public, and accessible by ferry from Alexandria bay in New York state, and from the river ports in Ontario Canada. An exhibition on the life of George and Louise Boldt is on display in the main castle, while the power house has a photographic display of life in the Thousand Islands region in the 19th century.

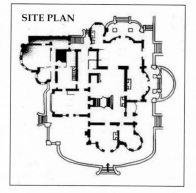

SITE PLAN

Elaborate windows and turrets of the main building.

Facing page:
Heart Island, on which the castle stands, was originally Hart Island, but the name was changed after the heartbreaking tragedy of 1904, which led George Boldt to abandon the project.

Bannerman Castle

Bannerman Castle is situated on Pollepel Island just off the eastern shore of the Hudson River, about 50 miles (80 km) upriver from New York City. It is an extraordinary pseudo-Scottish edifice, built in the earlt 20th century by Francis Bannerman IV, who ran a flourishing business in trading army equipment. His growing inventory required large amounts of storage, and New York City laws did not permit him to expand his warehouses within the city limits. The problem became acute after the Spanish-American War, when he was able to purchase immense quantities of the US Army surplus ammunition and stores. In 1900 Bannerman purchased the previously uninhabited Pollepel Island, and personally designed storehouses and a residential castle at the highest point.

The castle is a stone and brick edifice, decorated with archways, corner towers, turrets and corbeled windows that are profusely embellished. Various items from the army surplus stores have also been used in the decoration. A crenellated parapet runs around the roof perimeter. The legend 'Bannerman's Island Arsenal' was engraved on the side of the castle, and was clearly visible to passing ships that may have carried prospective customers.

ADDRESS	The Bannerman Castle Trust, Inc., P.O. Box 843, Glenham, NY 12527-0843
CONSTRUCTION HISTORY	**1901** Construction began
	1918 Construction ceased
	1920 munitions explosion
	1969 Major fire damage
	2009 Major wall collapse of the front and east wall
COMMISSIONED BY	Francis Bannernan IV
MATERIALS	Stone, brick
STYLE	Island castle; 20th-century American

Construction ceased after Bannerman's death in 1918, and two years later the complex was damaged in a huge explosion of powder and stored munitions. The island was abandoned in 1950, until purchased in 1967 by the New York state, which removed the military. A huge fire swept through the castle in 1969, and thereafter the island was banned to all visitors. In December 2009, nearly one-third of the castle suddenly collapsed.

According to native American legend and sailor's lore, Bannerman Island is haunted, which adds to its air of mystery. At present, the castle is owned by the New York State Office of Parks, Recreation and Historic Preservation. It is assisted in the task of preservation by the Bannerman Castle Trust, a voluntary organization begun by the descendents of Francis Bannerman. One of the aims is to stabilize the structures to make it safe for the public.

Facing page:
The main purpose of Bannerman Castle was to store munitions and army supplies, and the legend on its walls served as an advertisement for the owner's business.

Although in ruins, it is still possible to see the elaborate detailing in the arches, windows and parapets.

A dilapidated staircase leads to an equally derelict building.

Hearst
Castle

USA

Washington DC

United States National Historic Landmark

The spectacular Hearst Castle was built by Randolph William Hearst on a 127 acre (51 hectare) estate on a rocky slope, some miles inland of San Simeon Bay in California. It was a family camping ground with rustic lodging, and Hearst asked the architect Julia Morgan 'to create something a bit more comfortable.' Thus Camp Hill became 'La Cuesta Encantada' or 'The Enchanted Hill', and between 1922 and 1947, an array of opulent mansions were erected there in an amazing mix of architectural styles. Invitations to Hearst Castle were highly prized, and included the business and political elite of America in the 1930s, as well as the leading lights of Hollywood. Guests such as Charlie Chaplin, Charles Lindbergh, Clark Gable, Franklin Roosevelt and Winston Churchill arrived on Hearst's private train car from Los Angeles or were flown in on his personal aircraft.

The main house or the Casa Grande had 130 rooms, and three lavish guesthouses, namely Casa del Sol, Casa del Mar, Casa del Monte, were built for visitors. These were all in the Mediterranean Revivalist style with majestic Spanish towers. Hearst's private study was in the Gothic mode, while one of the suites was inspired by the Doge's Palace in Venice. There was a full sized theater that screened films from Hearst's movie company 'Cosmopolitan Productions'. There were abundant terraces and gardens, a series of outdoor pools, and an indoor pool resembling a Roman bath. Underground storage vaults for his massive art collection and other treasures were also incorporated into the design.

ADDRESS	Hearst Castle Road, San Simeon, CA 93452 USA
CONSTRUCTION HISTORY	**1922–26** Construction of Casa Grande
	1922–36 Pools
	1947 guesthouses, gardens, other facilities
COMMISSIONED BY	William Randolph Hearst
ARCHITECT	Julia Morgan
MATERIALS	Cement, steel, stone, brick, wood
STYLE	Palace-castle; 20th century American

The outdoor Neptune Pool.

The Hearst Corporation donated the estate to the state of California in 1957. It is now maintained as a state historic park, and receives nearly one million visitors each year. Among the highlights is the gilded and decorated ceiling at Casa del Monte, the Roman style mosaic floor in the foyer of the Casa Grande, and the statuary at the Neptune pool. Hearst's collection of priceless European art is also displayed in these elegant surroundings.

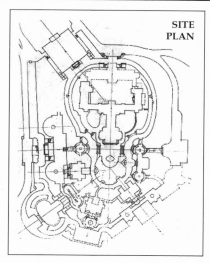

SITE PLAN

Facing page:
Opulent grandeur marks every aspect of the Hearst Castle, which was a statement of the owner's personal style, and an apt setting for his fabulous collection of European art treasures.

The dining room in Casa Grande.

WALES
Chepstow
London

Chepstow Castle

Chepstow castle is perched high on a narrow limestone cliff overlooking the river Wye in Gwent. It was one of a string of Welsh castles established by William the Conqueror in the 11th century and constructed byWilliam FitzOsborn. It secured the river crossing and provided a crucial staging point for armed forays into Wales by the English. The castle eventually passed to the Clare family. In 1115, the legendary William Marshal acquired the castle by marriage to the heiress Isabel de Clare. His sons considerably expanded the fortifications, but with the death of Anselm Marshal in 1270, Chepstow passed to the powerful Bigod family, who were Earls of Norfolk and kin to the Marshalls.

Chepstow has an unusual, elongated shape that follows the line of the limestone ridge. A rectangular keep separated the upper and middle bailey, by means of a narrow covered passage. Roger Bigod III added the formidable Marten's T ower to the southeast wall, with its impressive living quarters and a chapel. It acquired its name much later in the 17th century after Henry Marten, a famous prisoner, spent 20 years in the tower for the crime of having signed the death warrant for King Charles I.

Though twice besieged during the Civil wars, Chepstow escaped major damage or slighting, and was turned into a garrison fort until 1685. It changed hands many times after that, and most of the buildings and walls fell into decay and neglect.

The ruins of Chepstow Castle besides the river Wye.

ADDRESS	Chepstow, Monmouthshire, Wales
CONSTRUCTION HISTORY	**1067–1071** Two-story Norman keep; an upper and middle bailey
	12–13th century Third floor added to the keep; a lower bailey with an imposing two-towered gatehouse, as well as a barbican to the upper bailey; external curtain wall completed
	1240 Marten's Tower
	1245–93 A second Great Hall and living quarters for the lord's family, with kitchen and latrine; covering of the passageway between upper and middle bailey; a D-shaped residential tower at the southeast wall, with pyramidal spurs for added strength
COMMISSIONED BY	William the Conqueror
BUILT BY	William FitzOsborn, Marshal family
MATERIALS	Limestone ,sandstone, brick, timber
STYLE	Linear castle; keep and curtain wall

Since 1984, it is managed by Cadw, the government agency in charge of Welsh historic monuments. Many annual events and festivals are staged here amid these historic ruins.

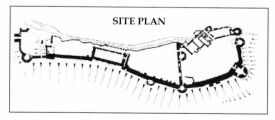

SITE PLAN

Facing page:
The outer gatehouse of Chepstow is protected by two imposing towers. Marten's Tower (at left), is easily distinguished by the pyramidical spurs at its base.

Intricate details are visible in the windows of the crumbling castle walls.

WALES
Pembroke
London

Pembroke Castle

Situated on a rocky headland, surrounded on three sides by the Pembroke river, his medieval castle's thickest walls were built on the side facing the town. The earliest structure here was an 11th century earth and timber fort built by Roger of Montgomery. In 1189, it was granted to William Marshal, who turned Pembroke into a powerful stronghold. The castle survived many battles and was an important base against Welsh rebellion until the mid-15th century. It reverted to the Crown in 1389. In 1457, while under the stewardship of Jasper Tudor, the castle was the birthplace of his nephew, the future Henry VII. During the Civil War, Pembroke declared for the Parliament and was unsuccessfully besieged by Royalist forces. However, its castellan changed sides in 1648, which led to its seizure by Cromwell's army, after which it was ordered to be slighted.

William Marshal constructed a triangular bailey and a giant cylindrical stone keep. With nearly 20 ft (6 m) thick walls, the keep rose to a height of 80 ft (24 m), and comprised five floors, including a basement. The top was domed, with two lines of crenellation. When attacked, wooden platforms were erected projecting outwards from the battlements. Gaps between the timbers were used to pour pitch, tar and stones on the attackers (in later castles, these became stone machicolations). Interestingly, a natural cavern beneath the castle, called the 'Wogan', served as a hideaway when the castle was under threat.

William Marshal's massive circular keep.

ADDRESS Pembroke, Pembrokeshire, Wales, SA71 4LA, UK

CONSTRUCTION HISTORY **1093** Earth and timber fortress by Roger of Montgomery

1189–1218 Inner bailey with towers, stone keep and outbuildings

1234-41 Outer wall extended to make second bailey, barbican and gatehouse with a machicolated vaulted passageway with three portcullis, stair turrets on the inner side of the gateway

1648 Outer towers partially demolished by gunpowder explosion

1880 Barbican rebuilt

1928 Extensive restoration begun

COMMISSIONED BY The Earls of Pembroke

MATERIALS Limestone, ashlar, timber

STYLE Linear castle

The castle remained abandoned till 1880, when it was acquired by J R Cobb, an enthusiastic antiquarian. In 1928, it was purchased by Major-General Ivor Phipps who undertook a 10-year restoration project. At present, the castle is jointly managed by the Phipps Family Trust and the Pembroke town council.

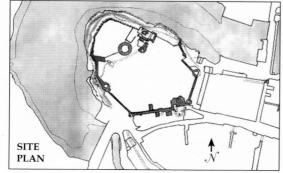

SITE PLAN

Facing page:
One of the strongest castles in Wales, Pembroke was identified with the powerful Marshal family in the 12th century.

An underground, natural cavern served as a hideoout and additional accomodation.

Conwy
WALES
London

Conwy Castle

UNESCO World Heritage List

Another one of the magnificent Welsh castles ordered by Edward I in the 13th century, Conwy impresses visitors by its majestic line of battlemented towers and its admirable location. It was constructed in just four years by the brilliant medieval military engineer, Master James of St George. Edward I was besieged at Conwy in 1295 by the Welsh rebel Madog ap Llywelen. However, supplies came in by the river and Edward rallied his forces to crush the rebellion. Conwy changed hands several times in the following centuries, and fell into disuse by the early 17th century. There was some damage at the hands of the Parliamentarians in 1655. A decade later, Lord Conwy allowed the castle to be stripped of its timber and iron.

In 1817, a river bridge was built next to the castle by Thomas Telford. A second bridge built by Stephenson came up in 1848.

The narrow castle follows the shape of a rocky outcrop bounded by the rivers Conwy and Gyffin. Extending outwards to enclose the town, the curtain wall has a total of 21 round mural towers along its perimeter, all of which are still standing. The citadel is reached from the town by a steep staircase, past three drawbridges and a well-defended barbican and gateway. The castle enclosure has eight towers, and a cross wall divides it into two baileys. The royal apartments, chapel and living rooms were in the towers of the inner ward, while the outer ward contained the kitchens, stables, and the garrison quarters. Besides the main entrance, there were two other posterns--a chapel postern and one exiting from the inner ward. An uninterrupted wall walk runs along the curtain, and all the towers have putholes to support wooden hoarding platforms.

Turrets and towers of Conwy with crennellations.

ADDRESS	Conwy, Gwynedd, Wales, LL32 8AY
CONSTRUCTION HISTORY	**1283** Construction of castle and town wall (*bastide*) begins
	1289 Construction completed
	17th century Castle falls into decay and neglect
	1655 Minor damage in the Civil War
COMMISSIONED BY	Edward I
ARCHITECT	James of St George
MATERIALS	Limestone
STYLE	Concentric castle

Conwy castle is an inscribed World Heritage Site, and a Schedule I listed building administered by Cadw.

Facing page: One of the best preserved of Welsh castles, Conwy's crennellated towers look much the same today as they did in the 13th century.

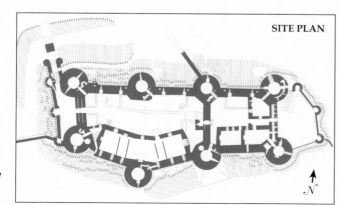

SITE PLAN

N

The circular gateway towers.

Caernarfon
WALES London

Caernarfon Castle

UNESCO World Heritage List

The mighty Caernarfon castle was constructed by the master builder from Savoy, James of St George, on the orders of Edward I of England following his conquest of Wales in 1283. Edward's infant son, who was born at Caernarfon in 1284, was invested with the title of Prince of Wales in 1301. Since then, the heir apparent, or the eldest son of the reigning monarch, has always received this title. In 1969, HRH Prince Charles was invested with the title of Prince of Wales at Caernarfon, in a televised event watched by millions.

Rising 98 ft (30 m) above the waters of the river Seoint, the imposing fortress looms over the busy town. The castle walls are strongly reminiscent of imperial Constantinople due to their turreted, multi-angular, mural towers and bands of colored masonry. From the northern side, they extend outwards to enclose the town in an uncommon English example of a *bastide* or walled town.

The castle has an unusual hourglass shape, with a cross wall dividing the upper and lower baileys. Nine towers and two twin-towered gateways protect the entire enclosure, and in case of attack, three tiers of archers stood at the *meurtrière* or murder holes in the battlements. In most strongholds, the wall walk provides easy access to all points of the castle for defenders and attackers alike. At Caernarfon, the towers sit astride the walk, so that portions could be closed off to the enemy. The upper bailey contains the Black Tower, the Queens Gate, the Northeast Tower and the Granary Tower. The lower bailey contains the Eagle's Tower, the Queen's Tower and the Well tower.

ADDRESS	Castle ditch, Caernarfon, Gwynedd, LL55 2AY UK
CONSTRUCTION HISTORY	**1283** Construction begins of castle and town wall (*bastide*)
	1330s Construction completed
	18th century Castle falls into decay and neglect
	1870s Restoration of the ruins by architect Anthony Salvin
COMMISSIONED BY	Edward I
ARCHITECT	James of St George
MATERIALS	Limestone, gritsone, siltstone (banding)
STYLE	Concentric castle

The internal buildings are mostly in ruins, though the external walls and towers are intact. The Royal Welsh Fusiliers Museum is housed in the castle. At present, it is under the management of Cadw.

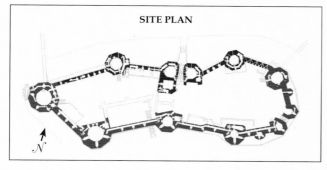

SITE PLAN

Facing page:
Designed to reflect imperial splendour, Caernarfon stands tall over the surroundng town and harbor.

The Eagle's Tower with the faceted walls which displays the typical banded masonry of the castle.

The elongated keep used to be divided by a cross wall at its narrowest point.

Harlech
WALES London

Harlech Castle

Majestic Harlech is among the several impressive castles built by Edward I to consolidate his authority in Wales. Designed by the foremost military engineer of the day, James of St George, this concentric fortress sits on a rocky escarpment overlooking Tremardoc Bay, ensuring a strong natural defense as well as constant supplies by sea. After its completion in 1290, Master James was appointed Constable of Harlech for three years. The castle was taken by the Welsh under Owain Glndwr in 1404, but was retaken by Prince Henry (later Henry V) in 1409. In the War of the Roses, Harlech was Lancastrian and surrendered to the Yorkists after a prolonged seven-year siege, an event immortalized in the song *Men of Harlech*. In the Civil War of the 17th century, it was one of the last strongholds to yield to the Parliamentarians.

Like all of Edward I's castles, Harlech was a feat of medieval military engineering with multiple lines of protection. The high-walled rectangular central keep has four stately corner towers. A second encircling wall, lower than the first, creates a narrow terrace-like outer ward. Another exterior wall enclosed the north and west side, traveling along the rocky escarpment down to the sea. Along it ran a fortified staircase to the water gate, which was an additional escape or entry point. The south and east side of the castle were protected by a moat. The eastern wall contained a mighty towered gatehouse, reached by two drawbridges. This formed a stronghold in itself that could hold out against external attackers, or internal threat from within the bailey.

ADDRESS	Castle square, Harlech, Gwynedd, UK
CONSTRUCTION HISTORY	**1285** Construction begins of castle and town wall (*bastide*)
	1290 Construction completed
	1647 Slighted by Parliamentarians in the Civil War
COMMISSIONED BY	Edward I
ARCHITECT	James of St George
MATERIALS	Limestone, gristone
STYLE	Concentric castle

The inner buildings are in various stages of ruin, but the towers and curtain walls have survived intact. At present it is administered by Cadw.

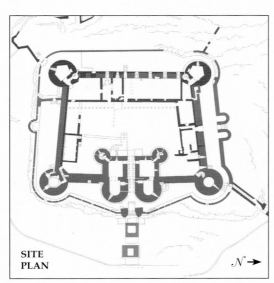

Facing page:
Framed against the peaks of Snowdonia, Harlech stands watch over the town and Tremardoc Bay.

SITE PLAN

N →

The imposing towered gateway that was a castle within a castle.

A covered passageway leading into the keep.

Beaumaris Castle

The last of Edward I's 13th century Welsh castles, Beaumaris contains all the classic elements of a concentric military fortification. Its name derives from the French *'le beau marais'* or 'the beautiful marsh', and it is located on flat marshy land on the Isle of Anglesey. Beaumaris was another masterpiece designed by the master builder James of St George, on a symmetrical plan similar to Harlech. The construction spanned 35 years, and involved an enormous amount of manpower and material. However, the castle was never completed as the Welsh threat dissipated, funds ran out, and Edward turned his attention to Scotland.

The outer curtain wall with 16 towers is lower than the inner curtain wall. Imposing corner drum towers and two formidable twin-towered gatehouses protected the inner bailey. In addition, there was a round tower at the center of the two remaining sides of the high curtain wall. The whole is surrounded by a wet moat fed by the Menai Strait. A protected tidal dock linked the castle to the sea, ensuring constant supplies, particularly during a siege.

Several lines of well thought out defensive elements included crenellations on the outer wall, murder holes or *meurtrière* in the passages, and machicolations on most of the battlements. A strategic misalignment of the entranceways on the inner and outer walls prevented straight access into the bailey. As the castle was never completed, the towers and gatehouses of the inner ward never reached their full height. The north gatehouse was intended to be 60 ft high with sumptuous royal apartments, but its top story was never constructed.

ADDRESS	Beaumaris, Anglesey, North Wales, SH 607 763
CONSTRUCTION HISTORY	**1295** Construction begins
	1330' Construction abandoned
	Late 14th century Castle falls into neglect and ruin
COMMISSIONED BY	Edward I
ARCHITECT	James of St George
MATERIALS	Grey and white stone, timber
STYLE	Concentric castle

Beaumaris escaped slighting and damage during the Civil Wars. It has survived the centuries almost intact, and is now in the care of Cadw. One of its highlights is the Chapel Tower which contains a fine Gothic chapel with a ribbed stone vaulted ceiling.

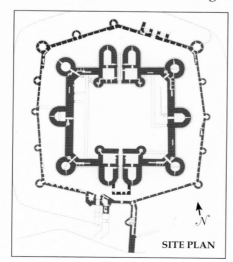

Facing page:
Beaumaris is one of the most romantic castles in Wales. It's almost perfect symmetry of design is typical of Edward I's 13th century castles.

SITE PLAN

The round towers of the curtain wall glow in the light of the setting sun.

One of the castle's arched passageways.

219

Additional Castles

AUSTRIA

Hochosterwitz, St Veith an der Glan
13th century, mountain castle, donjon and curtain
Archbishop of Salzburg

Rappotenstein, near Zwettl
12th century, mountain castle
Von Kneuringer family

Aggstein, near Melk
13th century, mountain castle
Von Kneuringer family

Forchtenstein, near Weiner Neustadt
14th century, mountain castle
Counts of Mattersdorf

ENGLAND

Restormel Castle, Cornwall
12th century, ringwork
Robert of Mortain

Tattershall Castle, Lincolnshire
15th century, water castle, donjon and curtain
Ralph Lord Cromwell

Herstmonceux Castle, Surrey
15th cnetury, water castle, Tudor
Alnwick Castle, Northumberland
12th century, bailey and keep

Alnwick Castle, Northumberland
12th century, bailey castle
Barons of Alnwick

Castle Rising, Norfolk
12th century, keep
William d'Aubigny

Hever Castle, Kent
13th century, walled bailey

Lewes Castle, Surrey
11th century, double motte and bailey
William of Warenne

Lincoln Castle, Lincolnshire
11th century, William the Conquerer

Skipton Castle, Yorkshire
11th century, walled bailey and keep
Baron Robert de Romille

Colchester Castle, Essex
11th century, city castle, donjon and curtain
Bishop Odo

Hedingham Castle, Essex
12th century, donjon and curtain
Count Aubrey de Vere

Colchester Castle, Essex
11th century, city castle, donjon and curtain
Bishop Odo

Conisborough Castle, Yorkshire
12th century,
donjon and curtain
Hamelin Plantagenet

Corfe Castle, Devon
12th century,
donjon and curtain
King Henry I

Framlingham Castle, Suffolk
12th century, curtain wall and bailey
Roger Bigod, Earl of Norfolk

Hever Castle, Kent, England.

Warkworth Castle, Northumberland
12th century, Tower house

Richmond Castle, Yorkshire
11th century, donjon and curtain

Rochester Castle, Kent
12th century, Harbour castle, donjon and curtain, Bishop Gundulf of Rochester

Portchester, Portsmouth
12th century, Harbour castle, donjon and curtain

Kenilworth, Warwickshire
12th century, Harbor castle, donjon and curtain, Geoffrey de Clinton

FRANCE

Château d'Haut-Koenigsbourg, Alsace
12th century, rock castle

Donjon de Niort, Poitiers
11th century, double donjon and curtain wall, Henry II of England

Chateau de Chamont, Chamont-sur-Loire
15th century
Chateau de Langeais, Langeais,
15th century, city castle
Louis IX

Coucy-Le-Chateau, Picardie
13th century, mountain castle,
donjon and curtain wall
Enguerrand III

Aigues-Mortes, Languedoc-Rousillon
13th century,
city castle
Louis IX

Salses Castle, Peripgnan
15th century,
artillery castle
Ferdinand II

CROATIA

Veliki Tabir
12th century, rock castle
Ratkaj family

CYPRUS

Kyrenia Castle,
12th century, crusader caste
De Lusignan family

CZECH REPUBLIC

Prague castle, Prague
10th century, city castle
Kings of Bohemia

Zvikov Castle, Pisek
13th century, rock castle
Kings of Bohemia

DENMARK

Nyborg Castle, Fyn Island
12th century, coastal castle
Kings of Denmark

Vordingborg, Zeeland
12th century,
island castle
Kings of Denmark

Donjon de Niort, Poitiers, France.

Hammershus, Bornholm
13th century, bailey castle
Archbishop of Lund

GERMANY

Kaiserburg Nürnberg, Bavern
11th century, city castle, donjon in curtain wall
Emperor Frederick Barbarossa

Münzenberg, Hessen
12th century, bergfried
Kuno von Hagen

Drachenfels, Konigswinter
12th century, bergfried
Archbishops of Cologne

Wildenberg, Odenwald
12th century, palace-castle with bergfried
Rupert von Dürn

Rheinfels, near St Goar
13th century, rock castle
Counts of Katzenelbogen

Lichenstein, Bavaria
13th century, ganerbenburgen
Lords of Lichenstein

Schönburg, Oberwesel
12th century, rock castle, ganerbenburg

HUNGARY

Castle Eger, Eger
13th century, rock castle
Bishops of Eger

Pataki Vár. Sárospatak
15th century, city castle

ITALY

Castel Roncolo, Bolzano
13th century, rock castle,
donjon in curtain wall
Heren of Wanga

Rocca Maggiore, Umbria
14th century, rock castle, tower, curtain and bailey
Cardinal Albornoz

IRELAND

Limerick Castle, Limerick
12th century,
city castle
King John of England

ISRAEL

Chastel Pèlerin
13th century, coastal castle
Knights Templar

Montfort, Mi'ilya
13th century, rock castle
Teutonic Knights

LATVIA

Sigulda Castle, near Riga
14th century,
curtain wall and bailey
Teutonic Knights

NETHERLANDS

Kasteel de Haar, Haarzuilen
12th century, water castle
Gotschalk of Woerden

NORWAY

Akerhaus Castle, Oslo
13th century,
rock castle
Haakon V Magnusson

POLAND

Ksiaz Castle, Lower Silesia
13th century, city castle
Bolko I

Wawel Castle, Cracow
11th century, city castle
King Boleslaw Chrobry

Limerick Castle, Limerick, Ireland.

PORTUGAL

Braganza Castle
12th century, city castle, Sancho I

Elvas Castle
13th century, tower, donjon and bailey
Kings of Portugal

ROMANIA

Hunyad Castle, Hunedoara
14th century, rock castle

SCOTLAND

Threave Castle, Kirkudbrightshire
14th century, tower house
Earl of Douglas

Craigmillar Castle, near Edinburgh
14th century, tower house
Simon Preston of Gordon

Claypotts Castle, Tayside
16th century, tower house
John Strachan

SLOVENIA

Predjama Castle
13th century

SPAIN

Alcazaba de Almeria, Almeria
10th century, rock castle
Abd al-Rahman II

El Real de Manzanares, Madrid
15th century, mountain castle
Don Iñego López de Mendoza

Guadamur Castle, Toledo
15th century, *torre del homenage*,
curtain wall

Torrelobatón Castle, Castile
15th century, *torre del homenage*,
curtain wall
King Juan II

SWITZERLAND

Schloss Tarasp, Tarasp
11th century, rock castle

Thun Castle, near Bern
12th century,
donjon and bailey
Dukes of Zähringen

Gruyères Castle, Fribourg
11th century,
donjon and bailey
Counts of Gruyère

Grandson Castle, Vaud
11th century, donjon and bailey
Lords of Grandson

SYRIA

Safita Castle,Tartus
13th century, donjon and curtain wall
Knights Templar

Chastel Rouge, Qal'at Yahmour
12th century, tower and bailey
Montolieu family

TURKEY

Edessa, Urfa
11th century,
donjon and bailey
Knights Templar

Kyrenia, Girne
12th century, rock castle
Lusignan family

WALES

Caerphilly Castle, Glamorgan, Wales, UK
13th century, water castle
Gilbert de Clare

White Castle, Gwent
12th century, curtain wall and bailey

Wawel Castle, Cracow, Poland.

Glossary

fre : french; spa: spanish; ger: german

Alcazaba (spa): Spanish term derived from the Arabic 'casbah' meaning the high place of the ruler. It refers to the citadel or official area occupying the high point of the city.

Alcázar (spa) : Spanish term derived from Arabic, meaning fortified palace. It is usually adjoining or close to the *alcazaba*.

Bailey: courtyard

Barbican : a forebuilding protecting a gate or entranceway, usually fortified.

Bartizan : a turret set high on a wall face, supported by corbels. It could be at the corners, or in the middle of the walls, or in the towers.

Bastide (fre): a fortified town

Bastion: a projection that gives a wider firing angle; a fortification

Batter: a wall thickened at its base to form a sloping face; talus

Belfry: a mobile siege tower

Berm: the space between a wall and ditch or moat

Bergfried (ger): a tall tower, not necessarily for residence.

Bombard: large siege cannon for destroying walls

Breastwork: a low defensive wall rapidly constructed in battle

Bretèche (fre): a stone machicolation over a doorway or window

Bulwark: a projecting work usually made of earth

Buttress: a vertical stone reinforcing strip for a wall

Castle: derived from the Latin *castellum*. Also called *château* (fre), *burg* (ger), *castello* or *castel* (ital),*zamek* (polish),spanish (*alcázar*), hrad (czech) grad or gorody (Slavic)

Castellan: the governor or caretaker of the castle

Caponier (fre): a covered passage across a ditch, also used to defend it

Casemate: a bombproof vaulted chamber built in the thickness of the rampart

Châtelet (fre): gatehouse

Chemin de ronde (fre)*: a wall-walk

Chemise (fre): a skirting wall around a motte, usually without a tower in the 12th century to create a shell-keep.

Concentric: a castle built with rings of mutually supportive walls

Corbel: a stone or wooden supports for bartizans or machicolations

Crenel: the open section of a battlement between merlons

Crenellation: a battlement

Curtain: a wall that encloses a castle

Donjon: a great tower or keep

Drum tower: round tower

En bec (fre): a tower beaked or pointed to the field

En bosse (fre): cut stone where the outer face is left rough(rustic)

Enceinte (fre): the defended area enclosed by the curtain of the castle, also used to denote the wall itself.

Escutcheon: a shield-shaped surface decorated with a coat-of-arms.

Fausse-braie (fre): a continuous low rampart or wall in the ditch in front of the main rampart.

Ganerbenburg: German castle shared by joint heirs of the same family

Garderobe Latrine

Gatehouse: A defensive work at the entrance of the castle usually with towers and barbican.

Glacis (fre): a smooth stone incline.

Gothic era: An architectural period from the 12th to the 15th century, characterized by high walls, flying buttresses and vaulting.

Gran buque: boat-shaped castle, such as Penafiel in Spain

Hoarding: wooden shuttering built out from the battlements to command the space at the foot of the wall; the wooden precursor to stone machicolation

Hornwork: an outwork

Keep: the most fortified part of the castle, called a donjon till the late middle ages. Square until the 12th century, after which it was also octagonal or round.

Loggia: a roofed gallery on the side of the building

Loophole: a slot in the wall through which an archer shoots

Lunette (fre): a detached semi-circular bastion forming a permanent outwork.

Machicolation: works added to a battlement which extend beyond the wall to allow material to be dropped through the gaps; initially temporary and wooden, then permanent in stone.

Mantlets: large wooden shields protecting foot archers and sappers

Merlon: the section of the battlement between crenels

Meurtrière(fre): 'murder hole' usually found in the ceiling of gateways to allow defenders to attack invaders from a hidden position, or pour water in case of a fire.

Moat: a ditch, either wet or dry

Motte: a mound of earth with either a tower, or a shell keep

Mural tower: a tower attached to, and usually projecting from the curtain wall (as opposed to a free-standing tower). The passages within would be termed mural passages.

Mudéjar (spa): A Spanish-Moorish style of architecture, with emphasis on decorative stonework

Outwork: A trench or fortification outside the main defenses

Pilaster: a flat buttress with little projection.

Portcullis: iron-shod wooden lattice that could be dropped to block a gate.

Postern: a lesser or private gate; sally port

Putlog holes: square holes in a wall face that secured horizontal scaffolding poles or beams for supporting hoarding.

Rampart: an earthen bank, often on the edge of a ditch, usually topped with a palisade or wall.

Reconquista (spa): The reconquest of Spain and Portugal from the Moors during the middle ages

Ring-work: a ditched enclosure without a motte.

Sainte-Chapelle (fre): name given to churches which enshrined a relic

Sally port: small gate used to escape or launch a raid or a sortie

Scarp: the inner side of a ditch

Shell-keep: a circular keep on a raised ground with a open space in the middle; also called keep without a tower.

Slighted: to damage a castle so that is can no longer be used for defense

Solar: Private chamber in a castle; usually the lord's private chamber and the well-lit room.

Spur: an angular projection from the face of the wall

Tenshu : the tower in a Japanese castle

Trebuchet: a siege engine

Très Riches Heures: A 15th-century illustrated Book of Hours of the Duc de Berry

Wall walk: passage running around the upper level of the inner perimeter of the curtain wall; *Chemin de ronde* (fre)

Ward: a courtyard, bailey

Framlingham Castle.

Picture Credits

Front Cover: Burg Eltz

p2 Andrew D Hurley (Flickr Creative Commons); p4 Amandajm (Wikimedia Commons); p6–7gatefold: Alhambra dome, Justus Hayes,(Flickr Creative Commons); Bodiam Castle portcullis,Brian Snelson, (Flickr Creative Commons); Castel Nuova, Naples ,David Holt, (Flickr Creative Commons); Stirling Castle kitchen (Wikimedia Commons); Dover castle chapel (Wikimedia Commons) p8 John Ford (Flickr Creative Commons); p9 Adam Cuerden (Wikimedia), BigDaddy1204 (Wikimedia Commons), Wyrdligh (Wikimedia Commons); p10 Cristof1887 (Wikimedia Commons); p11 ahsigett (Flickr creative Commons), Ignis (Wikimedia Commons), pinpin (Wikimedia Commons); p12 Thomas (Flickr ARR);p13 Viollet le Duc (Wikipedia), Charles Oman (Wikipedia); p14 Stacey Chapman (Flickr Creative Commons); p15 *clockwise* Xvlun (Wikimedia Commons), axiepics (Flickr Creative Commons), Canada cow (Wikimedia Commons), lostajy (Flickr Creative Commons), steve p2008 (Flickr Creative Commons), andy54321(Flickr Creative Commons), Semnoz (Wikimedia Commons); p17 *top* flo p (Flickr Creative Commons); *bottom* Allie Caulfield (Flickr Creative Commons); p18 Ana (Flickr Creative Commons); p19 *top* Coy! (Flickr Creative Commons); *bottom* Smabs Sputzer (Flickr Creative Commons); p20 LupusBXL (Panoramio); p21 *top* Phanatic (Flickr Creative Commons); *bottom* Viktorhauk (Wikimedia Commons); p22 Vince Alongi (Flickr Creative Commons); p23 *top* m.gifford (Flickr Creative Commons); *bottom* gamma-ray productions (Flickr Creative Commons); p24 Mario Groleau (Flickr Creative Commons); p25 *top* Airbete (Wikimedia Commons), *bottom* Goodnight London (Flickr Creative Commons); p26 Hotel Hukvaldy (Flickr ARR); p27 *top* Tibor Kádek (Wikimedia Commons), *bottom* Kazuo Ikeda (Wikimedia Commons); p28 Peter Lindsay (Flickr Creative Commons); p29 *top & bottom* Chiara Marra (Flickr Creative Commons); p30 Elena Pleskevich (Flickr Creative Commons); p31 *top* astique (Flickr Creative Commons), *bottom* Matěj Baťha (Wikimedia Commons); p32 duryno (Flickr ARR); p33 *top* vlastní fotografie (Wikimedia copyright free), *bottom* Robert Paprstein (Wikipedia); p34 David Ellwood (Flickr ARR); p35 *top* draco2008 (Flickr Creative Commons), *bottom* quinn norton (Wikimedia Commons); p36 James Trickey (Flickr ARR); p37 *top* Jo Jakeman (Flickr Creative Commons), *bottom* offwhitehouse (Flickr Creative Commons); p38 Jake Keup (Flickr Creative Commons); p39 *top* Jake Keup (Flickr Creative Commons), *bottom* Michael Rowe (Wikipedia); p40 Olivier Bruchez (Flickr Creative Commons); p41 *top* jimbowen0306 (Flickr Creative Commons), *bottom* A. Norppa (Wikimedia Commons); p42 Paul Reynolds (Flickr Creative Commons); p43 *top* Andrew Griffith (Wikimedia Commons), *bottom* waldenpond (Flickr Creative Commons); p44 James Byrum (Flickr Creative Commons); p45 *top & bottom* exfordy (Flickr Creative Commons); p46 Chuck Andolino (Flickr Creative Commons); p47 *top* Dave e smith (Flickr Creative Commons), *bottom* supermac1961 (Flickr Creative Commons); p48 Alex Brown (Flickr Creative Commons); p49 *top* Jo Jakeman (Flickr Creative Commons) *bottom* Glen Bowman (Wikimedia Commons); p50 Andrew Skudder (Flickr Creative Commons); p51 *top* Marcin Chady (Flickr Creative Commons) *bottom* dave pape (Wikimedia copy free);p52 Jim Crossley (Flickr Creative Commons); p53 *top& bottom* Karen Roe (Flickr Creative Commons); p54 (Wikimedia Commons); p55 *top* jooliargh (Flickr Creative Commons) *bottom* benjgibbs (Flickr Creative Commons); p56 Nic Gourlay (Flickr Creative Commons); p57 *top & bottom* nikoretro (Flickr Creative Commons); p58 Stephane Martin (Flickr Creative Commons); p59 *top & bottom* Man vyi (Wikimedia copy free); p60 Panoramas (Flickr Creative Commons); p61 *top* Rd Picard (Flickr Creative Commons) *bottom* Nitot (Flickr Creative Commons); p62 (Wikimedia Commons); p63 *top* Nitot (Flickr Creative Commons) *bottom* Pascal RADIGUE (Wikimedia Commons); p64 Sybarite48 (Flickr Creative Commons); p65 *top & bottom* Frank Wouters (Wikimedia Commons); p66 Alain Guichard (Flickr Creative Commons); p67 *top* Laifen (Wikimedia Commons) *bottom* tim herrick (Wikimedia Commons); p68 Casper Moller (Flickr Creative Commons); p69 *top* Allie Caulfield (Flickr Creative Commons) *bottom* Osbern (Wikimedia Commons); p70 Celbleu (Flickr Creative Commons); p71 *top* http 2007 (Flickr Creative Commons) *bottom* Christophe EYQUEM (Wikimedia Commons) p72 Patrick Carpentier (Flickr Creative Commons); p73 *top* Joseph Morris (Flickr Creative Commons) *bottom* 'Les Très Riches Heures du Duc de Berry' (Wikipedia copy free); p74 (Wikimedia Commons); p75 *top* Sémhur (Wikimedia Commons) *bottom* Manfred Heyde (Wikimedia Commons); p76 Panoramas (Flickr Creative Commons); p77 *top* al.pliar (Wikimedia Commons) *bottom* stephanemartin (Flickr Creative Commons); p78 Etienne Boucher (Flickr Creative Commons); p79 *top* Abderitestatos (Wikimedia Commons) *bottom* Wyzik (Flickr Creative Commons); p80 Martin Bravenboer (Flickr Creative Commons); p81 *top* db2r (Flickr Creative Commons) *bottom* AEngineer (Flickr Creative Commons); p82 Wolfgang Staudt (Flickr Creative Commons); p83 *top* Wolfgang Staudt (Flickr Creative Commons) *bottom* Marc Ryckaert (Wikimedia Commons); p84 MorBCN (Flickr Creative Commons); p85 *top* Philllip Capper (Wikimedia Commons) *bottom* Phillip Capper (Flickr Creative Commons); p86 Robert Scarth (Flickr Creative Commons); p87 *top* Fotograf Ingo2802 (Wikimedia Commons) *bottom* (Wikipedia copyright free); p88 Ralf Schulze (Flickr Creative Commons); p89 *top* Bo&Ko (Flickr Creative Commons) *bottom* Marfis75 (Flickr Creative Commons); p90 (also on cover) Markus Ram (Flickr Creative Commons); p91 *top & bottom* Turelio (Wikimedia Commons); p92 Rainer Ebert (Flickr Creative Commons); p93 *top* Rusty Boxcars (Flickr Creative Commons) *bottom* Luhai Wong (Flickr Creative Commons); p94 Xavier Sosnovsky (Flickr Creative Commons); p95 *top* (Wikipedia copyright free) *bottom* Nicolas von Kospoth (Wikipedia Commons); p96 Robin & Bazylek (Flickr Creative Commons); p97 *top* axiepics (Flickr Creative Commons) *bottom* shadowgate (Flickr Creative Commons); p98 Csaba Petrik (Flick ARR); p99 *top* Móni77 (Flickr Creative Commons) *bottom* Darinko (Wikipedia copyright free); p100 Molamoni (Flickr Creative Commons); p101 *top* uzo19 (Wikimedia Commons) *bottom* David Spender (Flickr Creative Commons); p102 Indiamike; p103 *top & bottom* Kartikeya Saigal; p104 Adrian Whelan (Flickr Creative Commons); p105 *top* Shivam Chaturvedi (Wikimedia Commons) *bottom* Kartikeya Saigal; p106

Facing page: Castle El Real de Manzanares, Spain.

Bindaas Madhavi (Flickr Creative Commons); p107 *top* anirudh (Wikimedia Commons) *bottom* Rudolf.a.furtao (Wikimedia Commons); p108 Shadowgate (Flickr Creative Commons); p109 *top* shadowgate (Flickr Creative Commons) *bottom* Erik Charlton (Flickr Creative Commons); p110 Chad K (Flickr Creative Commons); p111 *top* sal&sam (Wikimedia Commons) *bottom* Donaldytong (Wikimedia Commons); p112 Andrew Parnell (Flickr Creative Commons); p113 *top* William Murphy axiepics (Wikimedia Commons) *bottom* Laurent Espitallier (Wikimedia Commons); p114 Wimbledonian (Flickr Creative Commons); p115 *top* Richard Luney (Wikimedia Commons) *bottom* donna (Wikimedia Commons); p116 Kieran Lynam (Flickr Creative Commons); p117 *top* Jacopo O (Flickr Creative Commons) *bottom* (Wikimedia copyright free); p118 Verity Cridland (Flickr Creative Commons); p119 *top* Verity Cridland (Flickr Creative Commons) *bottom* vic15 (Flickr Creative Commons); p120 Susanna Fratarcangeli (Flickr Creative Commons); p121 *top* Yab994 (Flickr Creative Commons) *bottom* Harlock 77 (Wikimedia Commons); p122 Zongo 69 (Flickr Creative Commons); p123 *top* Scott Stensland (Wikimedia Commons) *bottom* Lalupa (Wikimedia Commons); p124 Minghe (Flickr Creative Commons); p125 *top* Giorces (Wikimedia copyright free) *bottom* Janericloebe (Wikimedia copyright free); p126 Slowpoke748 (Flickr Creative Commons); p127 *top* b.roveran (Wikimedia Commons) *bottom* pmorgan67 (Wikimedia Commons); p128 David Sanz (Flickr Creative Commons); p129 *top* & *bottom* Corpse Reviver (Wikimedia Commons); p130 Joop Dorresteijn (Flickr Creative Commons); p131 *top* Mshades (Flickr Creative Commons) *bottom* (Wikimedia copy free); p132 Riga Castle, Panoramio; p133 *top* Fearless Fred (Flickr Creative Commons) *bottom* Ashley R Good (Flickr Creative Commons); p134 Keith Yahl (Flickr ARR); p135 *top* & *bottom* Zongo69 (Flickr Creative Commons); p136 Yazan (Flickr Creative Commons); p137 *top* upyernoz (Flickr Creative Commons) *bottom* Peripitus (Wikimedia Commons); p138 cangaroojack (Flickr Creative Commons); p139 *top* Fmohod (Flickr Creative Commons) *bottom* Chmee2 (Wikimedia Commons); p140 Dave (Flickr Creative Commons); p141 *top* & *bottom* Christophe. Finot (Flickr Creative Commons); p142 Martin Morris (Flickr Creative Commons); p143 *top* Ellywa (Wikimedia Commons) *bottom* Mararie (Flickr Creative Commons); p144 Alistair Young (Flickr Creative Commons); p145 *Top* Jan Mehlich (Wikimedia Commons), *bottom* Sir Gawain (Wikimedia copyright free); p146 tomasz przechlewski (Flickr Creative Commons); p147 *top* & *bottom* hr.icio (Flickr Creative Commons); p148 Dortoka (Flickr Creative Commons); p149 *top* & *bottom* Am_(Flickr Creative Commons); p150 Paolo Perry (Flickr Creative Commons); p151 *top* & *bottom* Orium (Wikimedia); p152 Jorge Louzao Penalva (Flickr Creative Commons); p153 *top* andrea.prave (Flickr Creative Commons) *bottom* wilbanks (Flickr Creative Commons); p154 Gaspar Serrano (Flickr Creative Commons); p155 *top* Beata Jankowska (Wikimedia Commons) *bottom* Elena Chochkova (Wikimedia Commons); p156 Jenni Douglas (Flickr Creative Commons); p157 *top* Zoonabar (Flickr Creative Commons) *bottom* (Wikimedia Commons); p158 Paul Stevenson (Flickr Creative Commons); p159 *top* & *bottom* (Wikimedia); p160 Eusebius (Flickr Creative Commons); p161 *top* Adam Cuerdan (Wikimedia Commons) *bottom* shadowgate (Flickr Creative Commons); p162 Stirling Castle (Wikipedia Commons); p163 *top* David Monniaux (Wikimedia Commons) *bottom* randysonofrobert (Flickr Creative Commons); p164 Max Khokhlov (Flickr Creative Commons); p165 *top* Dr Janos Korom (Wikimedia Commons) *bottom* József Süveg (Wikimedia Commons); p166 Le Grand Portage (Flickr

Creative Commons); p167 *top* Rochester Scouser (Flickr Creative Commons) *bottom* Lars Ploughman (Flickr Creative Commons); p168 Viajesmag; p169 *top* Ra Smit (Wikimedia Commons) *bottom* Javier Carro (Wikimedia Commons); p170 MnGyver (Flickr Creative Commons); p171 *top* & *bottom* Nicolás Pérez (Wikimedia Commons); p172 Frank Kovalchek (Flickr Creative Commons); p173 *top* Alaskan Dude (Flickr Creative Commons) *bottom* kyezitri (Flickr Creative Commons); p174 (c) Josep Cors, Corsair Landings; p175 *top* & *bottom* pablo.sanchez (Flickr Creative Commons); p176 P. Medina (Flickr Creative Commons); p177 *top* Zoser (Wikimedia) *bottom* rahego (Flickr Creative Commons); p178 P. Medina (Flickr Creative Commons); p179 *top* & *bottom* Harmonia Amanda (Wikimedia Commons); p180 Wil van Otterdijk (Flickr Creative Commons); p181 *top* Alexandru Baboş (Wikimedia Commons) *bottom* Percita (Flickr Creative Commons); p182 Håkan Nylén (Flickr Creative Commons); p183 *top* (Wikimedia) *bottom* Wolfgang Sauber (Wikimedia Commons), engraving (Wikimedia); p184 Christoph Hurni (Flickr ARR);p185 *top* tm-tm (Flickr Creative Commons) *bottom* Pterjan (Flickr Creative Commons); p186 Eric Hill (Flickr Creative Commons); p187 *top* Ioan Sameli (Flickr Creative Commons) *bottom* Pear Biter (Flickr Creative Commons); p188 Charles Roffey (Flickr Creative Commons); p189 *top* & *bottom* ian.plumb (Flickr Creative Commons); p190 Ed Brambley (Flickr Creative Commons); p191 *top* watchsmart (Flickr Creative Commons) *bottom* Locer (Flickr Creative Commons); p192 Delayed Gratification (Flickr Creative Commons); p193 *top* Mewes (Flickr Creative Commons) *bottom* michel benoist (Wikimedia Commons); p194 Sue Kellerman (Flickr Creative Commons); p195 *top* Argenberg (Flickr Creative Commons) *bottom* Darwinek (Wikimedia Commons); p196 Ferdi (Flickr Creative Commons); p197 *top* Georges Jansoone (Wikimedia Commons) *bottom* bazylek100 (Flickr Creative Commons); p198 Quasimime (Flickr Creative Commons); p199 *top* dougtone (Flickr Creative Commons) *bottom* ks focalpoint (Flickr Creative Commons); p200 Dan Dvorscak (Flickr Creative Commons); p201 *top* Salim virji (Flickr Creative Commons) *bottom* Ken From NY (Flickr Creative Commons); p202 Jill Clardy (Flickr Creative Commons); p203 *top* david.nikonvscanon (Flickr Creative Commons) *bottom* Bernard Gagnon (Wikimedia Commons); p204 Terry Winter (Flickr ARR); p205 *top* joannelummy (Flickr Creative Commons) *bottom* maggie loves hopey (Flickr Creative Commons); p206 Athena (Flickr Creative Commons); p207 *top* Mr Phil Price (Flickr Creative Commons) *bottom* Haversack lit (Flickr Creative Commons); p208 Allan Harris (Flickr Creative Commons); p209 *top* David Benbennick (Wikimedia Commons) *bottom* vix B (Flickr Creative Commons); p210 Andrew D Hurley (Flickr Creative Commons); p211 *top* Fwiffo (Flickr Creative Commons) *bottom* Effervescing Elephant (Flickr Creative Commons); p212 The Moog (Flickr Creative Commons); p213 *top* Gwen Hitchcock (Wikimedia Commons) *bottom* pyntofmyld (Flickr Creative Commons); p214 Hamish Fenton (Flickr ARR); p215 *top* Richard0 (Flickr Creative Commons) *bottom* The Ancient Brit (Flickr Creative Commons); p216 neiljs (Flickr Creative Commons); p217dynamomosquito (Flickr Creative Commons); p218bastique(Flickr Creative Commons); p219bazylek 100(Flickr Creative Commons); p221 Squeezyboy (Flickr Creative Commons); p222 pablo.sanchez (Flickr Creative Commons).

Site / Floor plans throughout - Copyright reserved for each individual castles.